THE KEYS

Also by Denise Marek

THE KEYS

OPEN THE DOOR
TO TRUE EMPOWERMENT
AND INFINITE POSSIBILITIES

DENISE MAREK
AND SHARON QUIRT

HAY HOUSE, INC.
Carlsbad, California • New York City
London • Sydney • Johannesburg
Vancouver • Hong Kong • New Delhi

Published and distributed in the United States by: Hay House, Inc.: www
.hayhouse.com • *Published and distributed in Australia by:* Hay House
Australia Pty. Ltd.: www.hayhouse.com.au • *Published and distributed in the
United Kingdom by:* Hay House UK, Ltd.: www.hayhouse.co.uk • *Published
and distributed in the Republic of South Africa by:* Hay House SA (Pty), Ltd.:
www.hayhouse.co.za • *Distributed in Canada by:* Raincoast: www.raincoast
.com • *Published in India by:* Hay House Publishers India: www.hayhouse
.co.in

Editorial supervision: Jill Kramer • *Design:* Tricia Breidenthal

Library of Congress Cataloging-in-Publication Data

Marek, Denise
  The keys : open the door to true empowerment and infinite possibilities /
by Denise Marek and Sharon Quirt.
     p. cm.
  ISBN 978-1-4019-2296-2 (hbk. : alk. paper) 1. Control (Psychology) 2. Self-
esteem. 3. Self-realization. I. Quirt, Sharon, 1965- II. Title.
  BF611.M27 2009
  158--dc22
                                                2009002476

ISBN: 978-1-4019-2296-2

12 11 10 09   4 3 2 1
1st edition, July 2009

Printed in the United States of America

Enter here
all ye who
seek freedom.

CONTENTS

FOREWORD

*What would your life be like without the
distractions of negative thoughts, fearful feelings,
and that insecure voice that's preventing you from
bringing out your very best? Have you ever considered
what you'd do if you knew you couldn't fail?*

We know from history that unless we're challenged, human nature has a tendency to settle for mediocrity. But the gnawing dissatisfaction that led you to reach for this book won't let *you* settle. By picking it up, I believe you're ready to answer these questions from your heart; you're ready to choose to explore possibilities that would otherwise be lost. Congratulations! It's an act of courage to explore new avenues; it's an act of faith to acknowledge that you want your life's journey to be more than the day-to-day hamster wheel that keeps you running in circles.

What I've learned from my own work as a holistic physician, what has been reaffirmed by reading this book, and what *you* will learn; is that the *natural* state of the body and of life is one of peace, joy, and vibrant health. Anytime you respond differently—physically or otherwise—no matter how clear your intentions or how strong your determination, there is something *deeper* going on. How many times have you read a book, taken a class, or attended a workshop with the conviction that you'll change your life, only to find yourself stuck again a few weeks later? Why does this keep happening? The answer actually lies in the subconscious mind.

The primary function of the subconscious mind—the part that we don't control—is survival. The subconscious regulates our body's basic functions, ranging from blood pressure, hormones, immunity, digestion, and detoxification to muscle tone and aging. As part of that regulatory job, the subconscious protects us from emotional experiences and memories that are too painful, scary, or challenging to handle in the moment. This part of us doesn't "choose" or "judge" in any creative or logical way. It's a safety valve, never processing or integrating those traumatic experiences into long-term memory.

Dr. Joe Dispenza, who has spent the past decade researching and writing about the neurological functions of the body, says that the brain doesn't know the difference between imagination, memory, or reality. Whenever we begin to react on an emotional, biochemical, structural, and spiritual level to our life's experiences, we're being activated through a filter of perception or subconscious limiting beliefs. Consequently, we *reenact* those limiting beliefs developed as a result of the traumatic experiences by doing the same thing over and over again, not knowing how to, or why, we can't break the vicious cycle of pain, fear, and stress.

Let me share an example: You and your significant other have a trivial argument. As a result, you find yourself sinking into a deep depression. You're not sure why you're so down, but you feel helpless to respond to the experience any differently. Is there something wrong with you? Absolutely not! Your subconscious mind is filtering your perception through the lens of an earlier experience that was too traumatic, scary, or challenging to handle. On a conscious level, you may not be able to recall the exact incident, but the tape of the previous experience is replaying subconsciously every time you and your partner argue.

When you find yourself in a rut or afraid to move in one direction or another, no matter how much you *want* to, it's those same subconscious limiting beliefs, those confining thoughts, that are keeping you in the rut. As Louise L. Hay stated in her seminal book *You Can Heal Your Life:* "Everything begins with a thought, and a thought can be changed." Being able to recognize that those thoughts and *reactions* stem from the subconscious mind is a key component to transcending the perceived limitations hindering you from truly living a passionate and fulfilling life. And the keys for doing that are now in your hands.

In this book, Denise Marek and Sharon Quirt teach you to unlock your subconscious so that you can release the resistance keeping you from experiencing the power of the infinite universe and your infinite mind. The book contains practical tools and strategies for living an extraordinary life; and provides you with a blueprint for taking full responsibility for your health, career, finances, relationships, emotions, habits, and spiritual beliefs.

It's through the keys outlined in this book—those of *awareness, acceptance, forgiveness,* and *freedom*—that you'll step forward onto a path of practical and positive growth. Armed with this information, you'll be able to unlock your heart and align your actions in congruence with your authentic self.

Making lasting changes is hard work. It takes commitment. If you're looking for shallow, quick fixes, you'll need to look elsewhere. This book will help you learn to live more consciously, to summon the courage to embrace those parts of yourself that you've been denying, and to solve the deep challenges you haven't yet been able to figure out. You'll learn ways to make important changes in your life, both large and small, so you can become the powerful person you were always meant to be. You're holding *the keys*—so enjoy the journey!

With Infinite Love & Gratitude,
Dr. Darren R. Weissman,
the author of *The Power of Infinite Love & Gratitude*

INTRODUCTION

Open the Door to True
Empowerment and Infinite Possibilities

Wouldn't it be wonderful if you could find the keys to unlock the door to your full potential and free yourself from the negative chatter in your mind? What if you could find the keys that would release you from your past pain, fears, and feelings of failure? Suppose for a moment that there were keys that would open you up to immense joy and inner peace: Could you imagine what your life would be like if these keys existed? They do! They're within *you,* and with them you'll be able to open the door to *true empowerment* and *infinite possibilities.*

We've joined together to help you find these keys within yourself; your task is to use them. The rewards for doing so are tremendous. You'll be able to finally resolve any part of your past that's causing negativity around you. You'll better understand your life situation and enable yourself to remove the barriers that once stopped you from achieving your goals. You'll discover how to make positive changes and to systematically create the kind of life you've been longing for. You'll gain a brighter outlook on your future and a renewed zest for living. These keys will allow you to discover who you truly are and to become who you were born to be.

To assist you on your journey, the book is divided into four chapters:

Chapter 1: *The Key of Awareness*
Chapter 2: *The Key of Acceptance*
Chapter 3: *The Key of Forgiveness*
Chapter 4: *The Key of Freedom*

The first three chapters provide you with keys that open your life up to true empowerment. The first one—awareness—will allow you to free yourself from ego's control. You'll learn what the ego is, how it was formed, and how it manipulates you. You'll also discover how to conquer it by making yourself capable of all that you desire.

The second key—acceptance—will help you release all negative judgment toward yourself and others. You'll finally be able to accept yourself fully for who you were, who you are now, and who you can become.

You'll also learn how to accept others and to discover where you've judged and why.

The key of forgiveness is the third one. This will let you free yourself from the past. You'll discover how to take the positive lessons forward with you on your life journey and leave the painful emotions behind. Guilt, blame, anger, grudges, and other negative feelings will be released with this key. You can use it to discover whom to forgive and how to forgive yourself and others.

With the first three keys, you'll then be able to move on to the fourth and final one—freedom. This opens the door to infinite possibilities. You'll discover that you can create the life you've longed to live and become the person you were destined to become. You'll learn to live in honesty, to feel proud of yourself, and to control your ego.

Throughout each chapter, you'll also find italicized statements. These are designed to change your thought patterns in an empowering way. Choose the ones that resonate with you, write them down in a notebook, and refer to them daily—doing so will help you maintain a positive focus.

At the conclusion of each chapter, you'll be provided with the opportunity to reflect on what you've learned. These pages will guide you through the questions necessary to take what you've read and adapt it to your own unique situation. Give yourself a tremendous gift by doing the work. To acquire the keys, you've got to allow yourself to digest, understand, and apply what you've learned to your own life. Self-growth doesn't happen overnight. It takes time to get there; it's a process.

The written word is powerful, so write down your self-reflections instead of just mulling over what you've learned in your mind. That way, you can go back after you've finished the book and reread the pages you've written. Those alone will be enough to confirm to yourself that you've moved forward—you've become aware of ego's controls, you've accepted and forgiven yourself and others, and you've moved into freedom.

Write your letter at the end of each chapter *before* moving on because each chapter contains knowledge that builds on the previous one. Therefore, doing the work will ensure that you're ready to continue learning.

Use this book as an ongoing tool. Once you've completed your first four self-reflection letters, refer back to the book, reread it, and write another set of letters. You'll be amazed by how the knowledge contained within these pages will resonate with you differently each time you go through it, because who you are and what you're experiencing in your life during your next reading will be different. Continue to write

xviii

as many self-reflections as you feel you need to peel back the layers upon layers of old thoughts, perceptions, and beliefs.

Know that the number of letters—along with the length of time it takes to complete them—will be different for everyone. For that reason, take your time and proceed at your own pace. Write as many as it takes for *you* to get to the core of who you truly are—to uncover your *authentic* self and find the *you* inside that longs to be revealed. You deserve to be free and to live a life of your own creation.

It's time to open the door to true empowerment and infinite possibilities—so let the journey begin.

CHAPTER ONE

THE KEY OF AWARENESS

USE THE KEY OF AWARENESS TO FREE YOURSELF FROM EGO'S CONTROL

I'm aware that ego is a perception of the mind created by what I've seen, heard, and experienced in the past. I'm free to believe my own thoughts and release ego's control.

A hummingbird flew into a garage through a door that had accidentally been left open. In trying to escape, the bird went to the window and was banging itself against the glass. Even when all of the remaining doors were opened and freedom was just a few yards away, the bird kept beating its wings and bumping its little body against the invisible barrier.

If you were to watch the bird unsuccessfully trying to get out through the closed window, you might be baffled by its foolishness. How could it continue to throw itself against the window and not realize that what it was doing wasn't going to work? It would seem ridiculous. Yet isn't it true that many people find themselves in similar predicaments? When feeling stuck in an unsatisfactory life situation, rather than stepping back for a moment and looking around for an open door, a new opportunity, or a way to make things better, they continue to throw themselves into the same barriers, repeating negative patterns.

The reason they do so is that they believe the things they think, such as: *I've got no choice. This is just the way it is, and there isn't anything I can do about it. Besides, if there were an open door, I couldn't walk through it. I don't have enough time or money. I'm not strong enough, smart enough, courageous enough, deserving enough, successful enough, or good-looking enough to do it. Even if I were—and if I did—what would other people think?* These kinds of beliefs create a lot of fear and keep many of us trapped in dark places, trying to escape through the same closed window.

Where do these self-defeating thoughts come from? They're generated by the ego. Some individuals associate the word *ego* with being egotistical or vain. As a result, they believe they don't *have* an ego. However, everyone does—all of us.

Simply put, it's that inner dialogue telling you what you think about yourself, about others, and about the world. The ego is made up of perceptions and beliefs formed in your past by other people's rules, religions, and beliefs. It's been part of you since childhood and has continued to be shaped up to this very moment. From the day you were born, your mind has been absorbing everything you've seen, heard, and experienced—all courtesy of other people's egos—and that's how your own was developed.

The reason you think about and perceive things in the way you do is because you were programmed to do so based on your experiences and the feedback you've received from others—your parents, your teachers, the media, the church, your neighbors, and everyone else you've ever encountered. For example, imagine that, as a child your parents regularly told you that you were very stupid and incompetent. As an adult, what do you suppose you'll believe to be true about yourself? You'll likely view yourself as being stupid and incompetent! You could be extremely bright, yet your ego would keep you fearful and insecure about your intelligence, based on what your parents taught you to believe about yourself in the past.

As another illustration, if you grew up in a household where everyone was judged by how they looked or how much they weighed, the chances are pretty good that today you'll judge yourself, as well as others, based on physical appearance. This may cause you to doubt your self-worth. Your internal dialogue will likely try to convince you to believe things about yourself such as: *I'm fat. I'm ugly. I'm not good enough.* When you buy into these kinds of thoughts, you're opting to let ego control you.

When that negative side of ego has control over your life, no good comes of it. It creates fear, doubt, guilt, regret, blame, jealousy, and anger. It keeps you imprisoned in past pain and blocked from your innate potential. It may cause you to be hateful and hurtful toward yourself and others. It can hinder you from achieving what you truly desire out of life and from becoming who you truly want to be. You may be scared by thoughts of being less than perfect and also doubt your abilities. You can be preoccupied, worrying about what everyone else thinks; and it can convince you to sabotage and abuse yourself—and others—physically, mentally, emotionally, and spiritually. This is a side of ego that no longer needs to exist within you. It's not serving you.

You can release yourself from a negative ego and develop a positive one that's loving and kind toward yourself and others; one that allows you to see yourself as capable of achieving all that you desire; and one that encourages, inspires, and builds you up with positive self-talk. A positive ego will enable you to live based on your authentic self—and to become who you were born to become. It will create peace, simplicity, and honesty. It will assist you in creating a life of infinite possibilities. *That's* the ego you want to develop.

It's important to understand that there's a huge difference between creating a positive ego and denying reality with positive thinking. For instance, imagine an optimistic woman who thinks that everyone just adores her, and nobody ever says anything negative to her or about her. Yet in reality, she's just not aware of what's going on around her. She's so absorbed in herself that she can't see anything else. She can't observe that those around her are aware that she's faking herself out, and they aren't telling her what they see because they don't want to burst her silly bubble. They're afraid she's too fragile and naïve—she's in denial.

Developing a positive ego isn't about living in denial, being naïve, or pretending everything is perfect. In fact, it's quite the opposite. It's about being aware of the truth, of what's working for you in your life, and what isn't. This also means realizing that you're capable of changing those aspects of yourself and your life that you feel the desire to change. That's not foolish or naïve at all—it's real, it's strong, and it's empowering.

Perhaps the notion of releasing a negative ego and shaping a positive one frightens you because you believe that the negative serves you—that it makes you powerful, strong, efficient, successful, and so on. Perhaps you think it drives you to achieve maximum personal and professional success. Those perceptions, however, are far from the truth.

The successes you've had in the past aren't the product of a negative ego; they're the result of the *fighter* inside of you. They're the outcome of your spirit's desires, your true authentic self, the identity that was born to you—the one that knows the purpose you're here to serve in order for you to be happy and fulfilled.

To illustrate the difference between negative ego and your spirit, consider the following scenario: You have a family to support and feel driven to stretch and reach your full professional potential in order to do so. That urge to succeed comes from your spirit—your true self. It's pushing you to achieve what you truly want, which in this case is to take care of your family.

Here's where negative ego appears. After recognizing your desire to thrive in your career, your ego chimes in: *What if I fail? What if I don't succeed? What if I can't take care of my family?* Those thoughts create fear, which is the engine that powers the ego. It gets ego started. The "what-if" scenarios that result tend to negatively affect your ability to succeed. They cause you to doubt your capabilities. If you're fortunate enough to make it in spite of the fear, it's because your spirit is stronger than your ego. Sadly, for many people, that's just not the case. What often ends up happening is that the fears become reality. You're much better off releasing a negative ego.

Using the key of *awareness* will assist you in creating this release. It will help you regain control over your thinking, let go of your negative ego, and *re*program your mind. In the rest of this chapter, you'll discover where ego (and when we use the term *ego* from this point forward we're referring to the negative aspect of it) has been manipulating you in your life—physically, emotionally, spiritually, and mentally. You'll pinpoint the perceptions that have been blocking you from becoming who you were truly born to be. You'll become aware of the beliefs and opinions that no longer serve you in a positive way and learn how to let go of them. You'll free yourself from ego's control so you can be the true, authentic *you*.

BECOME AWARE OF WHEN
YOUR EGO WAS FORMED

> *I'm aware that at birth, my ego was like my
> speech—untrained. I know that with time it was
> developed, and with this awareness I can change
> that training, just like learning a new language.*

To understand how your ego gained so much control over you, you need to become aware of when your mind was programmed and when your ego became most entangled in your consciousness.

From Birth to Age 4

You enter this world without any issues, anxieties, or fears; you come with an untrained ego. However, starting on the day of your birth, you begin storing information. You may not remember anything that happened, yet during this block of time, your thoughts are being programmed by what you experience with your parents and by the things they teach you to believe. Additional programming comes courtesy of other family members, friends, religious institutions, television, and so on. In this vulnerable time, you're unable to say "no" to what you're seeing, hearing, or being exposed to. The experiences could be good, bad, or indifferent—in any case, they're not labeled or categorized. They're simply captured and stored in ego.

At this point, ego usually isn't controlling or manipulating you; it's not yet filtering on the level of consciousness. Instead, it's absorbing information, and it's being trained. What you learn in these years will play a significant role in shaping whom you become in the future. The experiences you have in this period can result in the development of certain issues that may affect you later in life, such as low self-esteem, trouble committing in relationships, or problems with obesity or anorexia.

Ages 4 to 10

These are the "experience" years—it's a time when you're open to absorb, learn, and try new things. You haven't quite grasped negativity yet, so you're most likely still playful and kind. You may have experienced trauma, but it hasn't stopped you from going out and trying again. You'll step over boundaries to see how far you can push them. You learn filters in this time, such as *No, I can't,* and *I won't.* Even though these filters are in place, you aren't able to control the emotions that drive you.

These are the years when you ask the questions: *Why? What? Where? How? When?* You ask everyone but yourself. You take in all of the answers and begin forming your own perceptions—your own ego. Whether it's created to be more positive or more negative depends on who surrounds you socially; what you're taught at school, by your religion, and at home; and how you interpret everything you experience. In other words, your external training is creating your internal perceptions. You're at a vulnerable point in your life, and you're forming your adult personality at the same time. During this time, you begin to learn fear. Ego is beginning to control your thoughts.

Ages 10 to 20

When you're in this age range, you've been programmed to believe who you are. You're aware of the fact that you're an individual, and you begin to really take stock of the things you like and dislike about yourself. To what extent the ego takes control of you depends on how you were raised, how your parents deal with their own egos, and how your teachers and religious leaders manage theirs, combined with everything you've witnessed and experienced up to this point. For instance, suppose you've been told for the last ten years that you're too short. Maybe now your ego says: *I'm too short, and I'm not good enough. I'm small, and I'm always going to be small and nobody's going to look up to me.* Your mind has already created that perception.

Maybe you overheard your gym teacher telling your math teacher that you were uncoordinated and awfully skinny for your age. You weren't meant to hear it, but you did. Well, in your mind, you begin to see yourself as small and not at all athletic. Your ego continually reinforces it by saying: *That's right! You're too tiny, and you're always going to be that way. You'll never be an athlete.* Even though you love sports, you'll probably give up because you'll replay those thoughts over and over in your mind. Have no doubt: your ego has a way of being very convincing. Your mind is programmed, and what you think are only perceptions.

Age 20 to the Present

From the age of 20 throughout the rest of your life, you either drop all of that past programming and become who you know yourself to be and live your authentic self, or you continue to be the person others have taught you to believe you are. If you live based on the second option, your ego has defeated you. Your warrior-self—the one who fights to maintain self-awareness, individuality, and self-preservation—is now defeated by the ego's control.

By this age, you're free from past influences. Whether you live with them or not, you're truly at a point where you can make changes that nobody but you can control. At this point *you* get to be the trainer of your mind. You're now at a time in your life when you can be free from all that was and create all that you need, want, and desire. You're capable.

BECOME AWARE OF HOW YOUR EGO MANIPULATES YOU

> *When my ego's voice is strong, I'm aware*
> *that I'm in control of the volume. I'm also*
> *capable of turning it off completely.*

Your ego will use fear to manipulate you. No matter who you are, if you're faced with fear—which can come under the guise of worry, blame, hate, guilt, revenge, and so on—it's because your ego is in control. To illustrate, suppose you're afraid of flying, but you need to get on an airplane. Your ego may tell you that you'd better not take the chance, because if you do, the plane will crash and you'll die. Your ego is going to come up with all sorts of disastrous scenarios in order to defeat you. Even if it's crucial for you to get on that flight because the trip is about making a significant advance in your personal or professional life, your ego will use fear to keep you put. If its voice is strong enough, you'll believe those thoughts and stop yourself from making the trip. At that point, your ego is in full control.

When this part of you has the upper hand, it can manipulate you in all areas of your life. It can affect your relationships, career, finances, health, and appearance, as well as your emotional, spiritual, and mental well-being. Imagine, for instance, that you're two years old and you witness your mother screaming at your father because he has come home late from work, he's spent all of his earnings, and he's drunk. The child that you are watches this episode and creates a mind-set that's fearful of that type of situation and behavior. That fear is placed in your ego.

Years pass by and you're married. Your spouse comes home half an hour late from work; and fear, jealousy, and anger automatically overcome you. Through the association of your past experience, you immediately feel that your partner has done something wrong. You look at your current situation and—because you were programmed as a child—you say, "How dare you show up half an hour late without calling me! Where were you? Who were you with? What were you doing?" Someone who hasn't had your childhood experience might simply ask, "Was the traffic bad?" Ego has just interfered in your relationship.

Even the way you love and accept yourself is controlled by ego. Suppose you're five years old and you hear your father telling your mother: "Boy, you sure are packing the pounds onto that behind of yours, aren't you?" You automatically place that comment about your mother's weight into your ego.

As an adult, you're in a relationship—or perhaps you're looking in the mirror, in a relationship with yourself—and you see that you've gained weight. Your ego will tell you things such as: *You're getting pretty fat, aren't you? You look horrible, don't you? Nobody is ever going to love you looking like that.* Once again, your ego is controlling you. It's manipulating the way you feel and think, and how you believe in yourself.

It's all programming. You think and behave the way you do because others have taught you to do so. It's all a state of mind that's created and generated through our past experiences. That's why you keep repeating negative patterns and coming up to the same road-blocks time and time again.

Now that you're aware of how ego manipulates you, the next time fear comes up and tries to block you from achieving, doing, and experiencing what you want, challenge your thoughts. Really take the time to stand back and examine where those self-limiting beliefs are coming from by asking yourself: *Why do I feel this way?*

For example, let's say you've been in a relationship with someone who is abusive or very negative, and you want to leave. Why are you still there? Why do you feel that you can't go? Is it because you're afraid that another person isn't going to want you? If so, why do you feel that way? Is it because you don't think you're intelligent enough, good-looking enough, or deserving of healthy love? Is it because you don't think you can take care of yourself on your own? Where did *those* thoughts come from? Did they arise from what others have told you or from past experiences? Did they come from what your partner is telling you now?

Questioning why you feel the way you do can be quite an eye-opener. It can help you pinpoint and understand where the negative thoughts originated.

This awareness will allow you to see that the opinions you're holding are neither factual nor helpful, and they usually don't reflect your current reality. They're simply perceptions you've adopted over time.

The good news is that they can be altered. Your ego is trained, so you have the option and ability to *re*train it. Just as you can take courses to change your profession, you can also change your mind. As you continue to read this book, you'll learn techniques for how to do so.

BECOME AWARE THAT YOU'RE CAPABLE

I'm aware that I'm capable. I'm able to defeat my ego and take control of it. I'm capable of accomplishing all that I desire. I'm capable of thinking for myself.

Your ego can control you, but it can also be controlled *by* you. If you want, you can have complete mastery over it because you always have the ability to create your own thoughts. You're free to think for yourself. You no longer have to buy into the beliefs that have been holding you hostage. Instead, you can acknowledge that you're an intelligent, worthy, and strong person who can accomplish great things in this lifetime. There are no limits or boundaries other than those you construct in your mind. Once you take control over negative perceptions, your ego can no longer stop you. You become free to reach your full potential.

To begin, tell yourself: *I am capable.* You *are* able to do anything you want to in this lifetime. In fact, list five things right now that you've already accomplished that you're most proud of. What are your five greatest achievements? You know what they are; you know what your accolades have been. You've succeeded in the past. That proves you're capable of doing so in the future.

You have a life of options and opportunities—we all do. You're capable of seizing those moments and doing what will bring you great joy and happiness. You're also capable of focusing on your desired outcomes and taking the steps necessary to achieve them.

There's no reason why you can't do what you want to do. As long as it's not morally, physically, or spiritually hurting anyone, you have the ability to experience all that you desire. It's simply your mind that influences you to think otherwise. Ego controls you. However, once you're aware of that, the easiest way to change it is simply to say: *I can. I'm capable.*

What do you really want? Would you like to move up in your career, improve your personal life, or enhance your financial situation? You're capable of journeying toward, and arriving at, whatever destination you choose. Regardless of what burdens you may have or what obstacles you're currently facing, you have the ability to overcome them. Sometimes it might take you longer than you'd like, but at other times, triumph occurs seemingly in the blink of an eye.

In either case, you must take the first step by believing (and thus making) yourself capable—capable of taking action, of studying, and of learning all that you need to in order to get to that next level. Others have succeeded, and you can, too. Whatever it is that you need to do in order to feel happier and more fulfilled, tell yourself: *I'm capable of that. I deserve it. I'm strong enough to do it. I believe I can—I know I can. In fact, I'm going to do it.*

Do you want to lose weight so that you can live in a healthier, stronger, leaner body? Can you do that if it's something you wish for yourself? Of course you can, because you're capable. You're capable of managing what you eat and changing the way you think about food. You have the ability to wake up every morning, open the fridge, and tell yourself: *I'm capable of choosing healthy foods and nourishing my body. I'm capable of drinking water, exercising, and loving myself more. I'm capable of making the positive changes I desire for my life.*

Do you want to be a doctor? Let's say you're a 42-year-old plumber but you've always wanted to be a physician. Are you capable of changing careers? Yes, you are. You still have at least 23 years of work ahead of you. Why don't you put yourself through school? If you've always wanted to do it, why not continue your career as a plumber for the next eight years while you train to become a doctor? Some people are graduating from college when they're 85 years old! How do they do that? It's because they've made themselves capable—and so can you!

What if you're 53 years old, all of your life you've wanted to be an architect, and you're aware that it's something you dream about even today? That realization is a *gift;* it's an open door inviting you to live your authentic self. Are you capable of walking through that door? Are you capable of becoming an architect? Of course you are; you always have been. Accept it.

The only thing that stops you is your ego. It's going to come up with an infinite number of reasons why you can't and shouldn't do it. It will tell you that you're not smart enough, you're too old, you're too broke, your kids are going to laugh at you, the neighbors will think you're crazy, and your partner will leave you. You'll come up with every single reason why you shouldn't take the steps necessary to achieve that goal. Admittedly, your ego's voice can be very strong at times. However, it's *you* who's in charge of the volume. Quiet down your ego by affirming to yourself that you're capable. By believing that truth, you defeat your ego's ability to render you incapable. As a result, you master it.

Remember, your ego doesn't want to be conquered. It wants to defeat *you,* so once again it will try to use fear to influence you. When it does, you need to regain control over your thinking and vanquish it. After all, you *created* it through the things you saw, heard, and experienced through others. It's not an alter ego; it's not something that sits on your shoulder. This voice was created by you; you just need to realize that you can control it.

First, examine the negative messages you're telling yourself. These unhelpful thoughts might include: *I can't do this. How dare I even attempt it? I'll never succeed.* Obviously, this line of thinking breeds doubt and can scare you out of taking the steps that could ultimately transform your life.

Then, as outlined in the previous section, identify where these beliefs might have originated by asking yourself: *Why do I feel this way?* Next, make yourself capable of taking action by replacing those negative thoughts with more nurturing truths. Tell yourself:

Excuse me, ego—I'm in control. I know what I want for my life, and I won't allow you to control the outcome. I'm in charge of that. I'm capable of making the positive changes I desire for my life. I can do it, and I will do it! That way, your ego won't be able to manipulate you with negative messages. In fact, you will have disturbed and eliminated it.

Don't be too surprised, however, if the next time you step outside your comfort zone your ego comes up again. It might say: *I did really well last time, but what if I fail this time?* You have the ability to switch it off again by replacing that negative self-talk with something along these lines: *I did a great job last time, and this time is going to be even better because I've learned so much more.* Changing your inner dialogue in this way will help give you the confidence to take another step in the direction of your desired outcome. In addition, the more you practice turning around that self-talk, the less hold your ego will have over you. You truly are capable of moving forward and progressing to your goal; once you're aware of that fact, you're in total control.

You're now aware of why and how your ego has controlled you and that you're capable of changing anything your mind thinks. Using these concepts, you can live an empowered life. You can be completely free of a negative ego at all times. You're capable of going to bed each night and confirming and affirming that truth.

This evening, tell yourself: *I am capable of waking up tomorrow and being a better person. I am capable of going to bed early tonight and not working so hard if that is what I need—or of staying up late and finishing this project and not being a procrastinator if that is best for me. I am capable of putting into my mind whatever thought it is that I need so that I wake up tomorrow morning as that better, stronger person.* Whatever it is that you want to be capable of, affirm it to yourself. It will change your life.

BECOME AWARE OF WHO YOU ARE

I ask my inner self: Who Am I? I answer from my true authentic self—not controlled by others' perceptions. Mine and mine alone is the only answer I will accept. I look into the mirror and I see a person capable and worthy of all I want and need.

In order to affirm *what* it is you want to be capable of doing and *who* it is you want to be capable of becoming, you first need to be aware of who you are without ego—without other people's perceptions, rules, and beliefs. Really take the time to discover who you are from within so that you can live your authentic life and be yourself. You don't have to go into the depths of meditation or hypnosis to do so; you simply need to do a self-diagnosis. Start by asking yourself: *Who am I?*

Look in the mirror, directly into your own eyes, and ask yourself that question. In your response, search beyond your physical appearance; look past the color of your skin and the shape of your physique. That's not who you are—it's only the body in which you reside. Avoid basing your response on who your mother, father, spouse, kids, employer, religious leaders, teachers, or society say you are or *should* be. Those are *their* perceptions, and the mission here is for you to discover who you are without ego. Besides, you're not what other people have thought about you in the past or even what they think about you now. You're *you*— be *you*. Live your *you*.

For the time being, seek for who you are beyond what you do to earn a living. While you might be an accountant, a CEO, a farmer, a factory worker, a professional athlete, a ditch digger, a police officer, a business owner, a dentist, or a firefighter, you're also an individual who's trying to evolve and learn how to become self-aware. Look beyond the roles you play in your family or society because while you might be a parent, a spouse, a child, or a neighbor, you're also a spirit—a soul—with its own unique identity.

Who is that individual within you? Who are *you?* Peel back the layers and uncover your authentic self. Reveal the individual you may have forgotten or who you thought was gone. Even if you feel lost right now, you're not. You're here. Maybe you're hiding from pain and those times you were burned in the past. Perhaps you don't want to look at the truth or all of the perceptions that made you think you weren't capable. Now, however, you know that you can do anything you want to do. You can make your life a better place as long as you take the time to find out who you are.

To get to the center of who you are, ask yourself this next question and listen to the answers that resonate with your spirit: *What makes me feel fulfilled inside?*

Pay attention to the things you do that feel good in your heart. For instance, perhaps you woke up this morning and walked across the street to take your neighbor a loaf of bread you'd baked because it makes you feel good to give to others. Maybe you gave of your time by spending an evening with an elderly person who was feeling lonely. If so, then you're a giver—that's part of your identity.

Perhaps you remember helping a woman when she burned her arm. You knew exactly what to do, and it healed. That felt wonderful. Then you recall that six years ago, you told someone with a throat infection which natural ingredient to use, and it cured her. Last year, you helped your mother recover when she hurt her neck. Well, maybe you're a healer. That could also be a part of who you are.

Create a list that describes you. These descriptions will all come together to create your one true identity. They make up the spirit that you are. It's also important for you to be aware of these aspects of yourself because individually, they're your purposes. Your inner self will feel so empowered once you discover them. Each of us is here to serve divine purposes, and you were born with the tools and knowledge to do so. Around the world, many cultures believe that we're on Earth to serve, to do a job, to give a gift from our spirit level.

There are many different purposes—teachers, directors, healers, and guides, just to name a few—and there are multiple subcategories of each and every purpose. Think about healers, for example. How many thousands of different types of healers are there? There are those of the body, mind, and spirit; different individuals work on physical, metaphysical, and psychological levels. The list goes on and on. Stop for a moment and ask: *What is it that I want, need, or must do in this lifetime? Am I a teacher, healer, guide, director, or something else? What is it that feels right for me?*

How many purposes are you here to serve? It depends. You might be meant to focus on one major purpose or on many. Only you have the answer to that question—and you *do* have the answers. They're within you. Find them by once again examining who you are without ego, exploring the things you do that fulfill you, and checking in regularly with your authentic self by asking: *What purposes am I here to serve?*

Additional clues to discovering your purposes can be found in your strengths, the things at which you excel. The reason is, as previously mentioned, you were born with everything you need—tools, skills, knowledge—to execute your purposes. As such, you'll have some natural abilities with certain things. Maybe you paint the most magnificent pictures or cook the most delicious meals; perhaps you're a powerful speaker, a talented athlete, or have an amazing mind for business. Those are gifts. They're there to assist you in taking on the various roles needed to fulfill your purposes.

You see, in order to carry out your missions, you take on certain functions. For example, if you're here to serve the purpose of teacher, you might take on the role of motivational speaker, author, coach, parent, or college professor. If your divine purpose is to be a healer, you might become a physician, a massage therapist, or a holistic practitioner.

To carry out your divine purposes, you must walk specific paths. Continuing to use a healer as an example, you may find yourself as a patient at one point on your path, as the friend of someone who needs medical attention at another, or with a partner who supports and encourages you while you attend school to earn your advanced degree. When you're aware of who you are ànd what your purpose is, you need to regularly ask yourself: *Am I on the right path?*

By doing so, you'll help ensure that you're on track. This self-reflection makes you consciously aware of the steps you're taking. By knowing who you are and what purposes you're here to serve, your authentic self will be in control of your life. The path you're on will be secure, safe, and empowered. You'll be aware of when your ego has nudged you off course and you're heading in the wrong direction.

Not all paths lead you where you need to go. That's particularly true when you're following a route created out of ego. Unfortunately, that's a road that a great many people find themselves traveling. One of the reasons is that for generations, society hasn't stopped to say: *Wait a minute. You don't have to blindly believe what I taught you. You go ahead and believe in what you choose to. Instead of following _my_ guidance, look to your inner wisdom. Rather than being who _I_ tell you to be, be _yourself._*

Too often, we're taught to be like everyone else instead of ourselves—to be who they are, to believe what they believe, and to think what they think.

Say, for instance, that one of your purposes is to be a spiritual teacher, and as a result, there's a longing inside of you to become a Buddhist monk. You have a strong desire to follow that path and take on that role. At the same time, your mother is standing in front of you saying: "I'm your mother, and I'm telling you to be a dentist. I'm a dentist, so you have to be one as well." If you fall into that ego trap, ignore your heart's desire, and become a dentist, the path isn't going to be pleasurable for you. You could have the most successful practice in the city and still come home at night and think, *What a crappy job.* That's because your authentic self knows that following your true path—taking on the role of a Buddhist monk—is what will help you fulfill one of your purposes and as a result, create peace, joy, and happiness. Yet you stay stuck in your job as a dentist and feel trapped, miserable, and unsatisfied. Anytime you experience those unfavorable feelings, go back and ask yourself the awareness questions: *Who am I? What makes me feel fulfilled? What is it that I'm supposed to do in this life? Am I on the right path to accomplish that purpose without ego's control?*

Is the track you're on right now based on your true identity? Is it leading you to become who you need to be in order to complete your purpose? If not, you're capable of changing your path. And you can do it regardless of society's opinions. It doesn't matter what anyone else thinks. If you're a doctor and you realize that in order to complete your purpose, it's important for you to become a plumber, who says you're not allowed to change? If you're in a controlling relationship and your true identity needs you to be free so that you can go back to school or do whatever it is you need to do in order to become the person you need to become, who can stop you from leaving? Who can stop you from switching tracks? If you can silence your ego, nobody and nothing will be able to stop you or tell you who to be.

Allow your spirit to decide where you go, not your ego. Let your higher inner guidance take charge of your life. You're capable. Affirm to yourself: *I can do anything I want to do. I can stay on this path or I can go. Whichever way it is, I am going to be capable of making my life a better place to be because I am free. I am free within myself to be honest with myself about what I want. What I need is to be who I am, not who anyone else wants me to be.*

Now that you've gone to the core of your authentic self and become aware of the roles and paths that help you carry out your purposes, take another look in the mirror and ask again: *Who am I?* Who do you see every day when you look at yourself? Do you see the same old person, or have you allowed your true self to be seen? Praise yourself for the evolution—you're becoming free from ego.

SELF-REFLECTION: WHO AM I WITHOUT EGO?

Today I'm aware of my ego, my true authentic thoughts, and my feelings. I'm aware that I control this life. I realize who I am and who I want to be. I recognize my inner-self and my need to grow. I'm aware of my past and that I can heal it.

You now hold the key of awareness. You're wise to the ego and its controls, and you're conscious of everything that you're capable of creating. It's time to reflect on what you've just discovered. One way to do so is to write yourself a letter of awareness.

The purpose of this letter is to reflect more deeply on—and to gain an even better understanding of—who you are without ego's control. Keep focused on that purpose by beginning with a declaration of your intention. This will keep you on track. Here's an example of a declaration of intention:

*My intention for this letter is to become
more aware of my true self without ego's control.*

With your intention in mind, use your letter to write down your answers to the following three questions:

- Who am I without ego's control?
- Who do I want to be?
- What do I want out of this lifetime?

Don't base your responses on what your mother, father, spouse, neighbors, teachers, or anyone else has taught you to be or has told you that you are. Answer based on who you know yourself to be—right now, in this very moment.

You know who you are. Were you born to be a spiritual leader, a teacher, a parent, a motivational speaker, a writer, and/or an artist? Were you meant to be a person who's loving and giving? Who are you? Here's one possible description: *I'm strong, capable, and wise. I'm very gifted and have great inner happiness. I'm emotionally open. I'm a good parent, and I'm proud of my children. I speak different languages, and I feel very good about that. I'm a healer and a giver.*

Keep in mind that you're the only person who has to read this letter, so it's safe for you to write the truth

31

about who you know yourself to be. Be completely honest with yourself. This means that along with focusing on your positive attributes, be truthful about the aspects of yourself that aren't 100 percent positive. Remember, this is *your* truth—what you know about yourself, not what others have told you.

Maybe you're going to be honest enough to say: *I guess I'm not a very good boss. I'm not very nice. I'm sort of hard on people.* Maybe your answer will be: *I'm a liar. I'm a thief. I'm a cheat. I'm a prostitute.* Whatever it is, answer honestly. What are your burdens? Are they controlling you? Is this what you want in your life, or do you dream of something better? Who do you want to be—a loving parent, faithful spouse, or trusted friend? You're capable of becoming that person.

Decide who *you* want to become. Perhaps you're a teacher and have always wanted to be a singer. Why not start taking steps toward that dream right now? What stops you? You can speak in front of a class; why not sing in front of an audience? Perhaps you've always wanted to be a veterinarian but you became a mechanic; or you've wanted to be an artist, but you're a police officer. Is there something you grew up long-ing to be, do, or achieve, but society, relatives, reli-gious leaders, teachers, and so on sculpted you into their molds? If you're aware that you still want to be something other than who you appear to be today, you can make that change. Don't let ego fool you into thinking you can't for one reason or another. Make yourself capable, and affirm it to yourself in this letter of awareness. Become that authentic self, and live that purpose. Follow your own heart.

Maybe you're already living in alignment with your true self. Perhaps you made the decision to be a dentist, and you have the awareness to say: *I like who I am. I'm so proud of the fact that every morning I get up, I go to work, and I'm helping somebody. I'm serving the purpose of dentist, which allows me to assist and heal others. I feel good about who I am, and my ego doesn't control that. It's the real me inside saying that I'm proud.* If you're pleased with the fact that you know what your purpose is and you're serving it well, write it down.

Begin achieving your desires by writing your letter of awareness. To help you get started, we've provided a sample letter to give you an idea of what yours might look like. Keep in mind that it serves only as a guideline. Your own letter will, of course, differ slightly or perhaps even significantly. You'll also notice that the example (as is the case with the remaining three sample letters in this book) is very general. All of your letters may be much more specific.

When writing your awareness letter (as well as the additional three letters you'll be prompted to compose in the upcoming chapters), choose a time when you can focus solely on yourself without outside distractions interfering with your thoughts. Clear your mind and concentrate on *your* feelings and thoughts. If any ideas arise that aren't about you, let them flow through your mind and then restore your attention back to the mission at hand.

Sample Letter of Awareness

Dear Self,

My intention for this letter is to become more aware of my true self without ego's control. As I'm reflecting on who I truly am, I'm looking at myself as I am today—not yesterday and not tomorrow—but right in this very moment.

I'm a human spirit, living a human existence. I see myself today as loving, playful, open, compassionate, passionate, youthful, beautiful, kind, giving, honest, peaceful, and thoughtful. I have a good mind and a big heart. I see myself as striving to be very healthy and as accepting who I truly am. I'm a gifted speaker and communicator. My strength as a powerful speaker—whether I'm presenting on stage, on television, on the radio, or even talking to one individual—allows me to heal, teach, motivate, and inspire others.

I know that I'm a teacher. I've regularly taught those I've been in contact with throughout my life. I'm capable of getting onstage and speaking in front of thousands. I've chosen this path in this lifetime to serve well. My ego isn't going to control it, and I'm not going to allow fear to control it. Instead, I accept that these are my true gifts and I'm thankful for them.

I'm aware that I've allowed my ego to control how I feel about my physical appearance. I've battled eating disorders in my lifetime. I've struggled to accept my body, and I've beaten myself up over even the slightest weight gain. I now know that ego was controlling me and manipulating me into believing that I had to be a certain size in order to fit into a culture that's very judgmental about physical appearances. I've come to the acceptance and awareness that regardless of my society's judgments and of my experiences of the past, I don't have to allow my mind to control me, making me think that I have to be a certain weight. I can choose to live comfortably, knowing that my body is fit and healthy. I'm now aware that I can be happy with who I am, regardless of my body size.

It's okay for me to continue to work on making myself physically healthy and fit so that I can fulfill my purpose and feel comfortable in my own skin. However, I now tend to my physical self because of my own desire to do so and not because of society's insistence that I be a certain size. I understand that now, and I accept it completely.

I'm also aware that throughout my lifetime, I jumped from relationship to relationship. I never took the time to really determine if I was in love with the person I was getting involved with. I never sat down to think about and determine whether or not I was happy, or if the relationship would enhance both of our lives. I'm aware now that I did so out of fear. I filtered my perceptions based on experiences in my childhood where I was denied love. My ego manipulated me with thoughts such as: You're lucky that anyone loves you at all. You have to stay in this relationship even if you're unhappy because if you leave, you're not going to be successful. You're not going to be financially secure. Nobody else is going to love you or want you, and you're not going to be who you want to be. *So I stayed with my partner until it became painfully clear that I was unhappy, or until I was afraid that my partner was unhappy and would soon leave. At that point, I'd jump right into another relationship because I was too afraid to be alone.*

I ended that pattern the day I realized that there was a part of me that hadn't yet been recognized. I wanted to get to know that aspect of myself. I wanted to get to know me without ego's control. I stepped out of a relationship with someone else and into a relationship with myself. When I did, I discovered that I was capable. I could live on my own and succeed. I found that my ego was wrong when it told me that nobody else would ever love me or want me. Someone did—and that someone was me. I want me. I love me.

Now I'm in charge of my mind and of my life—nobody else. I can be whoever and whatever I want to be. When I choose to be in a relationship, I'll enter into it as my authentic self and only if I believe the bond will enhance both of our lives. In addition, I'll no longer pretend that the things that make me unhappy or dissatisfied are okay. I won't shrink my inner light or give pieces of myself away. I won't pretend that things that make me feel left out don't matter. My thoughts and feelings are just as important as anyone else's. I can be honest with myself and with others about how I truly feel. I can be truthful about my needs.

I'm capable of honesty. Looking back on my childhood, I'm aware of how my ego was programmed based on some of the negativity and lies I had to endure. However, at this point in my life, I've come to terms with this. Who I am without ego is an honest person. I'm now capable of being truthful with myself and with others because I know that it best serves me and the universe in which I live.

I can see how ego was manipulating my ability to do this in the past. For the longest time, I wasn't honest about how I was truly feeling, what I liked and disliked, and what I wanted and didn't want. I lied so much and for so long about how I felt inside that I didn't even know that I was lying anymore, and I started to believe the things I was telling myself. My ego took control and said, "It's true. You really feel this way."

I've learned to survive without my ego's manipulation and control. I'm now living my purpose and using my gifts. I'm my authentic self, and I'm living with my own truth—the freedom in my spirit to know that I'm no longer captured within the pain of the past.

I'm aware that a lot of that anguish came from negativity in my childhood. Some of those early experiences created the belief in my mind that if I wasn't perfect, I wasn't lovable. Therefore, I did my best to project a perfect image. It was never enough, and I was certain that there was something wrong with me. I now know that there was never anything the matter with me—the only thing that was off-kilter was my ego manipulating my thoughts. I was just trying to be loved, to be accepted, and to find ways to fit in.

I'm also aware that throughout my life, I've had a tendency to become a "character" for others in order to help them feel happy. I find great joy in making others laugh and feel good about themselves and their lives. That's okay as long as I'm being authentic—as long as I'm being the kindhearted, caring, thoughtful, and giving woman that I know myself to be.

However, I can be honest enough with myself to know that sometimes that character is not my authentic self—it's an exaggeration of me. Sometimes I use this disguise to hide my true self in order to be accepted, liked, and loved. Now that I'm free from ego, I know that I don't have to exaggerate who I am. My authentic self is already all of those things—funny, caring, kind, giving, and fit— without having to put on an ego-driven façade.

I'm now aware of who I am: I'm me. I'm myself. I'm a speaker and a teacher. What I want out of this lifetime is to share my knowledge and experiences with others. To do so, I choose to become the best teacher I can possibly be. I'm aware of what I've accomplished so far, and I know what I want to learn next. I'm conscious of the steps I need to take in order to grow. I let go of my ego and the fear. I'm aware that within myself, I have all of the tools I need to survive and thrive. I'm capable of living my "me."

🔑 🔑 🔑 🔑

CHAPTER TWO

THE KEY OF ACCEPTANCE

USE THE KEY OF ACCEPTANCE
TO RELEASE NEGATIVE JUDGMENT

> *I no longer judge myself with the perceptions*
> *created by others. I'm self-loving, self-accepting,*
> *and aware of who I truly am. I've released negative*
> *self-judgment, and I am in control of my ego.*

Now that you're aware of who you are without ego, you may have come to the realization that you've been on the wrong path. Perhaps you see that you haven't

41

been living as your true authentic self, or you've discovered that you've held yourself in a negative pattern for many years. Maybe you've become aware of the fact that you've had low self-esteem, made mistakes, or sabotaged yourself throughout your entire life. Perhaps you don't like the person you've become.

Listen, you *are* okay. The fact that you're reading this now tells you it's the right time to make the right change. Accept that fact, because if you don't, your ego can manipulate you even more. And if that happens, you may find yourself even further off track a few years from now. That's what your ego wants, and it will use negative self-judgment to do so. Your ego gains tremendous power when you judge yourself from within. Believe it or not, it can even cause you to abuse yourself with alcohol, drugs, food, and other addictions, using all of its worst scripts! This is an internal battle: you versus the negative self-talk of your ego. That harmful voice will fight you to see how strong you are and how strong your spirit is. When you succumb to self-abuse, you end up judging yourself even more.

The arsenal of painful feelings that are born out of negative self-judgment (such as guilt, regret, sadness, and self-hatred) can scare you back into old patterns. These emotions can have you thinking that you should run back to your old life—return to being who you were when your ego was in charge. This is no surprise: the ego wants total control. It will work at proving that it's stronger than you are, but you know that's not true. You're doing the work; you're evolving. You've been making progress, so don't move backward. Keep going, keep growing, and accept yourself fully.

This means that you accept *who you were.* If you weren't living in alignment with your true purpose in the past, that's okay. Remember, back then you didn't have the tools or the awareness of how you were being manipulated, and now you do. Accept *who you are today.* You deserve happiness, joy, and peace. You're someone who's worthy of love and compassion from both yourself and others. Also come to terms with *who you can become.* You can now begin designing a life of your own creation. Begin to live your *you.*

This is what the key of acceptance will allow you to do. It will enable you to change the way you think about yourself and others. It will free you from the internal struggle that has thus far created obstacles and blocked you from living the life of your dreams. It will allow you to release all negative judgments and—as a result—accept yourself completely.

> *I'm a deserving person, and I'm capable of self-examination instead of negative judgment.*

You can—and you *deserve*—to accept yourself without conditions or judgment. Therefore, the first step in acquiring the key of acceptance is to become aware of how you've judged.

Examine this for a moment. How do you judge yourself? Do you do so based on how *you* feel about yourself or based on what *others* have said and what they've projected upon you? If you're like most people, it's probably the latter. For instance, suppose your father judged you as a child and said, "You're not very smart. You're really fat. You're always going to be fat." If you're now telling yourself those very same things, you're judging yourself based on his words.

Self-judgment is how we perceive what other people think of us and then how we view ourselves, based on that filter. To further illustrate this, suppose you're on a cruise ship and you're having a really great time. You and your partner are sitting at a dining table. At the next table, there's a couple that keeps looking back at you. Their glances are making you feel as though there's something wrong with you because your ego is present. You look down at your clothing and think: *Am I not suitable?* You check your hair and then your face to see if you have something out of place. You look at your partner and wonder: *Are we not well matched? What's wrong with us as a couple that they're looking back and placing their judgment upon us?*

Well, it's possible that they're not looking at you at all, but watching a television screen above your heads. Yet you're seeing their actions as judgment because you haven't yet experienced freedom from ego. It's in this moment that you need to use the keys of awareness and acceptance. Use the key of awareness to discover your ego's role in why you're feeling the way you do, and then use the key of acceptance to release the negative judgments and regain your inner peace.

If you don't use these keys, what do you think is going to happen for the rest of the trip? You're going to be looking around to see if anyone else is watching. You'll view yourself through critical lenses to determine if there's anything you need to be judged on.

Use the keys so that you're no longer sitting in a position of ego. Instead, look at the people you think are staring at you and internally say, *I accept you as you are, and I accept me as I am.* When you accept yourself, you end the judgment. As an added bonus, the other couple could suddenly acknowledge you with a nod and a smile and then return their gazes to the screen above your head, allowing you to realize what has actually happened! Your perception of the situation wasn't based on what was really going on. It happens—people often ruin great events in their lives because of the ego's control.

Even a wedding can be spoiled with judgment. Many women walk down the aisle thinking about all of the people staring at them. They're not focused on the moment in time that they're experiencing—one of the most joyous days in a couple's life. They're not thinking about how their hearts are feeling. Instead, they're worried about whether or not their clothes, hair, or flowers are perfect. They're wondering what other people are thinking. They're not really being in the moment because they're judging themselves—a self-judgment based on a *perception* of what others are thinking.

I'm in total control of how I view others. I choose to be free from negative judgments of myself and everyone else.

In addition to being aware of how you judge yourself, it's also important to realize how you judge those around you. Think for a moment about the word *lawyer*. What's the first thing you think of? Some people immediately think *sneaky, liar,* or an array of other unflattering descriptions. Many individuals are extremely judgmental based on just one word. Our egos are so connected to the unpleasant things we've seen, heard, and experienced that we're programmed to jump to the negative first. That's why it can be so difficult to be accepting—we make a hasty judgment based on an unfavorable state of mind. This is the ego's control, and it's a great manipulator.

In order to end the negative judgments and to be accepting, we need to change our perceptions. The reality is that there are a lot of lawyers who are fantastic people. They have incredible abilities and use their gifts to protect us. Many work for the underprivileged within a legal system that requires educated and reasonable counsel. Don't jump to the negative simply because of past programming. Become more aware and accepting.

Start processing everything in a new way by analyzing *first* with a positive mind-set rather than jumping straight to a negative viewpoint. When you choose to have the affirmative thought first, your ego can neither take control nor manipulate you. The positive perception creates a presence of mind that overcomes, controls, and defeats the ego.

If this is difficult at first, use a script to help you through. You can try something along these lines: *They're honest, good, and kind; and there's so much that's wonderful about them.* Granted, from time to time certain individuals may prove you wrong. At that point, you might view them differently because you know from *experience* that perhaps they really weren't all of those things you believed them to be. However, if they don't prove you wrong, they obviously deserved your positive judgment.

Analyze *yourself* in this way, too. Form opinions of yourself based on your generosity, kindness, and lovingness. Believe that you're empowered, strong, and intelligent. Accept yourself and know that you can go into this world and create anything you want to because you're capable of taking the steps necessary to get there every day. You're capable of fulfilling your purpose. When doing so—when you're serving your purpose—there's no need for you to negatively judge yourself

Tonight when you go to bed, say to yourself: *I'm going to positively analyze myself. I'm going to shift my thoughts and not focus on whether or not others will like my clothes or my appearance. I analyze myself through the positives first. I'm aware of who I am, and I accept it. I like me. I judge myself based on the fact that I love my work. I'm worthy and I'm capable.* Now you're analyzing yourself based on the positive presence of mind, not the negative ego stance. This changes the empowerment of your judgment. Your ego no longer controls it.

You've now acquired the key of acceptance. Use it to accept who you once *were* when controlled by ego, to accept who you *are* now, to accept who you can *become,* and to accept others.

ACCEPT WHO YOU WERE BEFORE YOU WERE AWARE THAT YOUR INNER EGO WAS IN CONTROL

I analyze myself in a positive way. I accept that although I've made errors in the past, I now realize they were lessons I needed to learn in order to serve in my self-growth. I'm capable of change and therefore won't allow those same errors to be part of my future. I accept that I've learned those negative lessons.

In accepting who you were, you need to accept that your life now and the person you are in this moment are both your creation. You are the result of the choices you've made in the past. How can you release the judgment if you don't like what you've created based on the choices of yesterday? Understand that you've made errors in the past, that you don't have to repeat them, and that you don't have to allow them to be part of your future. Remember, you're no longer that same person. You've evolved, and through your progress, you've become aware of how your ego controlled and manipulated you. You know now that you're capable of change.

What if you always wanted to be a pilot, but you believed that relative who said you weren't intelligent enough, so you didn't take the necessary steps to achieve your goal? First, you've got to accept that you allowed that situation to happen—you let the judgment of another block you from living your authentic self. You altered the course of your own destiny. It's okay; the past is over. There's still time to get back on track. Next, accept the fact that you're intelligent enough to become a pilot and do something about it.

Look back in time on your own life and reflect on the experiences where you really weren't being yourself—where you were living based on someone else's judgment. Suppose, for instance, somebody said, "You're really tiny. You're never going to amount to anything big because you're just too small." You grew up believing those things about yourself, feeling meek, unworthy, and incapable. But what if your purpose is to be a gifted massage therapist and assist people in releasing their physical pain? How do you overcome your fears and those mental obstacles so that you can fulfill that purpose? You need to free yourself from the judgment that's been placed there by the perceptions of other people by focusing on the positives—on your strengths.

Now that you know your strengths and what you really want to do, inside you might be saying: *I'm really good at that. I wish I could get out there and do it, but I'm so scared. I'm so afraid that people are going to judge me—my physical self, my decisions, and my intellect.* Thousands of people around the world have a great fear of stepping out and living their authentic lives because they don't yet have within *themselves* an acceptance of their true identity. They're judging themselves based on how they perceive others viewing them.

Your spirit has all of the tools and knowledge for you to be happy and truly serve your purpose. You have everything you require to survive and thrive. However, when you don't have the key of acceptance, you allow your ego to manipulate you with negative judgment, and you don't use your gifts. Instead, you hide and feel fearful.

For example, suppose you experienced trauma at birth, witnessing all kinds of negative events, and for one reason or another your parents were incapable of providing you with the guidance you needed to feel strong. Now your life is set up based on your feelings of being weak and unable to achieve what you truly long for.

With your new awareness, however, you're able to say: *My life doesn't have to be this way. I know this can change. I know I can take control because my limiting beliefs are the perceptions and lessons I've learned from other people. I'm reclaiming my identity.* When you do this, guess who's in charge? Your spirit. The inner self becomes more empowered. It's stronger, and it can take control of the ego.

ACCEPT WHO YOU ARE

I accept myself—mind, body, and spirit. I'm perfect in this physical self that I have. I'm growing and developing, and I'm becoming who I'm supposed to be. I accept that I'm worthy of my love.

You need to accept yourself—as the person you are—as you're developing. If you don't, your ego is going to manipulate you that much further and create great levels of negativity for your future. The ego can destroy both men and women, causing psychological, spiritual, physical, and emotional devastation. It can take you so far away from who you truly are that you end up feeling lost.

A prime example can be found in individuals who drastically change who they are in order to please and accommodate others. Imagine that a man overhears a woman telling her friend: "I'd love to meet a man who has a great smile, a successful career, and spends all of his time with me." The man really wants to have a relationship with this woman, so he gets veneers on his teeth, changes his career, and stops hanging out with his buddies. By trying to fit in, he's given up pieces of himself. He's no longer living *his* life. Somewhere down the road, he's going to become so out of tune with who he truly is that he'll become unhappy and resentful. At this point, the ego becomes empowered to take control.

Be proactive. Take the time to *know* who you are, *be* yourself, and *accept* yourself. You've spent enough time—under ego's control—trying to fit in and be accepted by others. You don't need that any longer. You must accept yourself because until you do, it won't matter how well others think of you. You'll keep judging yourself, and you won't feel as though you're ever enough. You *are* enough, though—exactly as you are in this moment.

Here's a way to do an honest self-evaluation right now: Ask yourself whether you accept yourself as you are today. Consider whether there are some aspects of yourself that you haven't yet come to terms with. Perhaps you haven't yet made peace with yourself on the intellectual level—you're not happy with your level of education or professional status. Maybe you're holding back on a physical level—you're not happy with your body, and you think that other people see you as fat. It could be that you don't like your hair, your nose, or whatever. If there's something about yourself that you haven't accepted yet, it's because your ego is controlling how you feel. That negative self-judgment arises from fear, and a lot of times it's just superficial.

Many such judgments are media driven. For instance, suppose a woman is 5'4" tall and weighs 135 pounds, but she sees herself as being obese. Why would she judge herself that way? It's due to past programming. Perhaps when she was a teenager, she was watching a movie with her boyfriend, and the leading actress was her height but weighed 110 pounds. Her boyfriend said, "Wow! She's gorgeous." Suddenly, the woman sees that image as perfect and herself as flawed. The media and marketing have played a huge role in the evolution of our egos.

We often think it's important to have the newest thing on the market—the latest car, phone, and so on. Marketing has programmed us well to want what it seems everybody else wants. Say, for instance, you have everything you really need: clothing, a car, a home, and food. However, you see that your boss or your neighbor has something that you don't—a more expensive car, a bigger house, a summer cottage, and a boat. Your ego may try to make you think that you're less important than these other people are because you don't have what they do.

You're equally capable of getting anything that anyone else has, but why do you want it? Is it because you need it to survive? Or is it because your ego tells you that you need it to be accepted? Over the years we've been *trained* to want what our peers have. This is where the saying "keeping up with the Joneses" comes from.

*I'm free to achieve what I need and want because
I am no longer allowing my ego to be in control.*

Until we can look at marketing and accept that a lot of the information that's being put out isn't truthful, the ego will maintain control. It will tell you not only to dress in a certain way, but that society *expects* it of you! The magazine you're reading this week says that red is in, so you get everything in red. Next week it says, "You need blue!" You think, *Oh no, I don't fit in. I'm not acceptable because I don't have blue.* We're so manipulated and controlled by ego, and most individuals aren't even aware of how deep it really goes.

Look at the booming business of cosmetic surgery. People get these procedures to adhere to a society- or culture-based definition of beauty. Our society—and psychology—suggests that a beautiful person will succeed more than a not-so-lovely person. So we might be tempted to change our physical identities in order to "succeed" in this face-value world.

> *I'm an authentic perfect being, and*
> *I accept who I am without change.*

No matter where you look, you have to admit that there's proof of what we're talking about. Every day, we're all experiencing this—from the animal kingdom to humankind. The prettier the feathers, the more we're attracted, just like birds in the wild. A person with a flashy car and large bank account appears to pull in mates, while someone with less can't even get noticed. Everything we do seems to be controlled in this way. If we're not doing well at work or at school, we feel that we're not as good as someone else.

Psychological studies around the world have helped marketers find ways of making us want to have the next best, biggest thing out there, including changing our appearance to get it. Do you really need to alter who you are to be accepted? No, you're capable of accepting yourself and making yourself as strong and efficient as you can with what you have.

I am capable of accepting myself as I am,
for what I have and for who I am becoming.

Are we suggesting that you should never get cosmetic surgery? Not at all. If you've decided to make changes to alter your physical appearance—whether it's through cosmetic surgery, weight loss, building muscles, wearing a toupee, or growing facial hair to cover scars—because you think you'd feel better about yourself, you can choose to do that. There's nothing wrong with it. Many individuals have chosen to make physical changes and have significantly enhanced the way they feel about themselves. That's wonderful. However, *before* you alter anything about yourself—whether it's your appearance, your career, or anything else in your life, for that matter—make sure you're doing it because it's right for *you.*

First, ask yourself: *Why do I think I should make this change?* Is it because someone else—a friend, an authority figure, or maybe the media—has given you a message that you should? Do you really want to alter who you are or how you look in order to be accepted by someone who's controlled by ego? Consider someone who says, *I'm quite fine, thank you very much. I'm not changing anything. I like the fact that I want a partner who's absolutely gorgeous; who has a perfect body, a perfect face, and a perfect career. That's just what I want.* They're being manipulated by their egos. Why would you alter yourself to be accepted by someone who's in this position? *You* have evolved. Don't fall into that trap.

On the other hand, when contemplating the reasons you think you should make a change, ask if it's because doing so feels right for *you.* Is it because you believe that making this change fits into the answer to the question *Who am I?* Is it because it will help you define the true you and become the self that's been hidden inside? That's a much better reason.

Next, change the word *should* to *could* and say to yourself: *I could make this change—so why haven't I done it yet?* Is it because you're afraid or think you can't? If that's all that's been holding you back—and the change is something you've determined is right for you—believe in yourself and remember that you're capable of taking steps toward creating the life you desire. However, if you realize that you haven't done it because it's just not something you want, by all means, drop it from your *should* list. In fact, get rid of your *should* list altogether and make a *could* list instead. It's much more empowering and offers peace of mind.

Many people live their lives trying to please others and meet outside standards. They beat themselves up for not being good enough because they've adopted someone else's opinion as their own. Decide today that you won't live that way. Declare that you'll make choices because they're right for you. Start living the life you desire for yourself.

I'm aware that I must learn from the invisible boundaries I've created in my life.

However, what if you've determined that you want to make a change, but you're unable to because of your financial situation? What if you're spiritually bound to a religion that doesn't allow you to make the change? What if you have a physical disability that doesn't permit the appearance you desire, or you're dealing with a disfigurement makes you see yourself as ugly? What then? *Shift your perception of perfection.*

You're already perfect exactly as you are. You were born a perfect being, and serving your true purpose keeps you that way. Your perfection comes from doing what you're meant to do and doing it very well. Somewhere along the way, you've just forgotten that it's *spirit* perfection, not *image* perfection.

Because it's obsessed with images, society can create a very negative type of control within the mind. Yes, it's good to be physically fit and to be conscious of your appearance, *but* make sure that the image you're presenting is created out of honesty. If you're going over and above what you want to do in order to be accepted and to fit in, you're creating a façade. Is that really perfect in any way? No. It's the opposite of perfect because you're not allowing yourself to be you.

After all, surface issues don't change who you truly are. The reality is, no matter how many modifications you make externally, you can't alter your *true* self. Sure, you can lose or gain weight, but you can't alter the structure of your inner being. Love your perfect spirit because when you do, you can then accept and love the "shell" in which it resides. You can embrace your round belly, your crooked toes, or the scars on your face. You can get to a place where you believe: *I may not be perfect from the media's perspective, but I most certainly am from the point of spirit because I serve myself with love. I'm free to love myself. I'm free to accept that I've created the outcomes in my life, and I'm free to serve my purpose.*

It's so much easier to live in self-love. There's no struggle. It flows; it's happy; it's joy. You'll achieve this by the end of this book. Self-love is freedom. Once you get to that point, other people's perceptions won't bother you anymore. What they think of you no longer matters because you know who you are, and you love yourself for it. As a result, you're no longer manipulated by anyone else's ego controls. You know from within what makes you happy, fulfilled, and ego free. Think your thoughts, and don't worry about what anyone, anywhere thinks—you're entitled to be yourself.

Be the *you* who says that you want to be a doctor instead of a nurse, or a nurse instead of a doctor. Why not accept yourself as you are? Just because someone else told you to be a doctor or a nurse doesn't mean that's what you have to be. If it's not right for *you,* you're selling yourself short. Be the individual who weighs 165 pounds and is five feet tall. As long as you know that you're content and healthy and that you completely love yourself at that weight, then that's okay. Accept the spirit inside of you who knows what will make you happy—where you'll be at peace and without internal struggle.

ACCEPT THAT SELF-SABOTAGE MAY BE ONE OF YOUR TRAITS

I now allow myself to embrace truth and happiness.
I am now capable of accepting my life path.

It's important to introduce the concept of self-sabotage here. Suppose you're out of shape, your doctor has warned you that excess weight is jeopardizing your health, and you say, *But I love and accept myself, so now I can gain more weight because my appearance doesn't change who I truly am.* That's self-sabotage. How can you fulfill your purpose and live your best life if you're not healthy? In this instance, your ego is back in control, and it's trying to convince you to abuse yourself. The ego is sneaky, and sometimes it takes a little more power to control it. You can say to yourself: *No, I'm not doing this. It's sabotage to allow my ego to direct my choices. I'm regaining control of my life. I'm capable of change.*

Humans sabotage themselves out of fear. Sometimes it seems easier and safer to stay just where you are. Essentially, you may tell yourself that it's harder to do the work and learn how to love yourself. Face it, change can be scary. If you aren't sure how your family, friends, peers, and co-workers are going to respond, it can feel like a risk not worth taking. You might start to believe that it's too tough to be aware of or accept what you're dealing with. Your ego will try to convince you to believe that the more difficult work comes with accepting yourself. It will firmly state that you might as well keep the negative judgments and just stay exactly where you are—safe and stuck. Don't fall prey to its sabotage. Outsmart it by analyzing yourself based on the *positives* first and in doing so accept who you *were,* who you *are,* and now who you can *become.*

ACCEPT WHO YOU CAN BECOME

I respect who I am becoming as I'm creating a better, stronger, wiser me. I'm listening to my inner self, and I'm learning. I'm empowered by my capabilities.

Have you blocked yourself with your own judgments? Have you stopped yourself from progressing because you don't believe you are worthy, capable, smart, or deserving? If so, accept that fact. But also acknowledge the fact that you want *better* for yourself—that you deserve better and that you're capable of making the change.

Once again, make sure you're becoming the person *you* want to be, not who you think you have to be in order to be accepted by others. Maybe you're looking at yourself right now, thinking: *I don't like the fact that I weigh 280 pounds. I don't like the fact that my hair is short. It used to be long and beautiful, and I used to take better care of myself. I don't like the fact that I wanted to be a lawyer; but I dropped out of school, got married, and now have a factory job that bores me to tears.*

The reason you're thinking those things about yourself may be that within your spirit, you know that you haven't continued on the path of who you were meant to be. The real you—your spirit—knows who you are and what you're capable of. It knows what purposes you're meant to serve, and it will keep nudging you internally to get back on track. As you learned to do in Chapter 1, continually check in with yourself to ensure you're making the changes *you* need, not because you're trying to fit into someone else's idea of perfection but because they're right for you.

If they *are* right for you, accept that you're capable of becoming who you want to be. It doesn't matter what anyone else believes to be true about you. All that matters is what you hold to be true. So if your boss says, "You'll never get past this level. We can't promote you because you're not smart enough. You're not what we'll ever need in the upper echelons," realize that's just her perception. Release her judgment so that you don't stay stuck. It doesn't matter what someone else says. As long as you accept who you are and what you're capable of achieving, you can move forward. You'll learn how to do this more easily as you work your way to freedom and acquire all four keys. Begin by believing you're capable, and then take the next step.

ACCEPT OTHERS

> *I accept others for who they are*
> *and myself for who I am becoming.*

You've learned to accept yourself for who you were, who you are, and who you can become. It's now imperative for you to also accept others for who *they* were, who *they* are, and who *they* can become. It's crucial for you to let go of the judgments you place on others because the more you judge them, the more you end up judging yourself.

Think of it this way: If you hold the belief that people who get divorced are immoral, that teenagers get pregnant because they have terrible parents, or that only failures go bankrupt, what does that make you if you get divorced, your child gets pregnant, or you end up in a financial situation where you have to declare bankruptcy? Does it make you immoral, a terrible parent, or a failure? No, it makes you an individual with lessons to be learned. However, if you've previously judged others on those issues, your ego will take hold and convince you that you should feel bad about yourself.

The reality is that we all have lessons to learn. The important thing to remember is that each of us is an individual. There's not one person in this world who can learn the way you learn or who can understand things the way you do. No one can think, feel, see, smell, or taste the way you do. It's not your purpose to judge anyone else for the lessons they need to learn or the ways in which they need to learn them. Your role is to accept them for who they are—unconditionally and without judgment. By coming to terms with *others* in this way, you become free to accept *yourself* unconditionally and without judgment.

We know this can be tough. When a judgment comes up, you can release it by saying to yourself: *Okay, wait a minute, that's a negative thought. It's judgmental, defeating, and based in fear. I'm not going to allow this to control me.* Then send acceptance to the person you were judging—acknowledge to yourself that this is a life lesson he or she needed. Remember, we all have things learn, and as individuals, we do so in different ways.

Suppose, for instance, that you're with two other people—one is an alcoholic and the other is morbidly obese. You realize that you're thinking negatively about them. Congratulations! You've just used the key of awareness: you're now aware that your ego is present. That's the first step in releasing the negative judgments. The next step is to use the key of acceptance: accept those individuals by realizing that where they are in this moment is a result of their own choices or perhaps even their diseases.

Don't negatively judge them for that. Instead, jump to the positive; acknowledge to yourself that they've made those choices in order to learn. The choices—the lessons—are theirs, not yours. Don't judge them for making decisions that are different from yours. Don't scorn them for not having the tools that you may have; they've received different ones. Accept that you're each unique and that you need to make your own way in this world just as they do. When you release judgment toward others, you release self-condemnation, too. You'll experience a new level of self-acceptance, you'll grow, and you'll become free.

Use the key of acceptance every day. For instance, imagine you're driving down the road and the man ahead of you brakes 25 feet before the stoplight. Your first impression might be: *What a jerk! Why did he do that?* You're negatively judging him for approaching a red light differently than you do. In that moment, the best second thought is: *I'm sorry for that judgment, and I send you a level of acceptance.*

Clear negative judgments you have about others on *all* levels: emotional, physical, spiritual, psychological, financial, intellectual, and so on. Even feeling sorry for someone is a form of ego. If you look at someone and think, *Poor you,* you're judging that in some way you're better than he or she is. You evaluate others based on how you see and perceive yourself. Perhaps you think: *They must feel sad because I have more—I'm taller, better, stronger, wiser, wealthier, or more attractive.* There's always a risk when you cast negativity on others that they in turn may place judgment upon themselves, thus continuing the powerful cycle of ego.

Accept everyone for their mind and their abilities. You must do this in order to free yourself. Remember, when you judge others on any level, you're actually acting on yourself. We're all equal—no better and no worse. Release the judgment, and forgive yourself.

SELF-REFLECTION:
WHOM DO I JUDGE, AND WHY?

*Today I'm accepting of who I am. I'm at peace
with my true thoughts, my true feelings, and my
true inner self. I embrace my need to learn from
the past and my new self-awareness. I accept my
gifts for all that I have and all that I am.*

You now possess the key of acceptance. It's time
to reflect on what you've learned and write yourself
a letter of acceptance, which will help you come to
terms with yourself and with others fully and unconditionally. In order to accomplish this, you first need
to identify *whom you've judged* and *why.*

Do you judge yourself—your appearance, intelligence, success, or goodness? Write down every
instance you can think of when you viewed yourself
negatively. Then ask yourself: *Why?* Are you critical
about your appearance because someone once told
you that you were too fat, too skinny, too short, too
tall, or unattractive? Are you judging yourself as unin-
telligent because you've always wanted to earn a college degree but you didn't go to school because you
didn't think you were smart enough? Why was that?

Did somebody somewhere tell you that you weren't successful because you didn't pass a certain exam or because you got 90 percent but your parents said it should have been 99 percent? Are you judging your success based on the fact that you've achieved something and now believe you're better than others, or is it that you've failed and now feel less than others? Write down all of your self-discoveries.

As you do so, keep in mind that those condemnations are coming from what you've seen, heard, or experienced in the past. In other words, they're based on ego-driven perceptions. If you only judge yourself based on ego, you'll never allow yourself to see your true spirit. Start looking at yourself from a positive view. Begin analyzing yourself based on your kindness, your generosity, your honesty, and the difference you make in the lives of others by serving the true purpose of your identity. Base it on what you know you're capable of achieving and who you're capable of becoming—that's important. Once you know you're capable and you no longer negatively judge yourself, nobody else's hurtful input will matter because you'll know who you truly are. Understand that you're just as capable as everybody else of taking the steps necessary to create the life you want and to become the person you want to become.

Do you judge others? Who? Are you frowning at someone walking down the street because that individual is 100 pounds overweight and you're at your ideal body weight? Well, it could be that he has a medical disorder, or maybe he's just accepted himself for who he is. Perhaps that person hasn't learned how to be accepting or aware of who he really is or who he wants to be. In any case, who are you to be the judge of what another human should be? You're no better and no worse; you're equal to everyone else.

Why is it that you're judging someone in the first place? Is it because you actually feel self-critical? Maybe it's because even though you're at your ideal body weight, you have a similar issue. Perhaps you secretly battle with an eating disorder, and you're projecting your own feelings about yourself onto that person. Are you evaluating the woman who, in your opinion, has had too much to drink because you have an issue with alcoholism? Are you condemning a person who's homosexual because you have a bisexual tendency? Are you dismissing a lawyer as being dishonest because you struggle with being truthful? Stop judging others in a negative way, and start looking at potentially who they really, truly are. Maybe those people are also very kind, loving, honest, and giving individuals who have helped many others throughout their lives. The more positively you analyze those around you, the better you'll feel about yourself.

Identify whom you judge and why in the body of your letter and then write statements of self-acceptance. Accept who you were before you were aware that your ego was in control. Accept who you are today. Accept others for who they are, and yourself for the person you're becoming.

Begin your letter with a declaration of intention such as this:

*My intention for this letter is to become
more accepting of my true self without ego's control.*

Sample Letter of Acceptance

Dear Self,

My intention for this letter is to become more accepting of my true self without ego's control. With that in mind, I ask myself: Whom have I judged, and why?

I'm aware that I've been judged and that I have judged. I once condemned all the members of my family for not accepting me and my truth. I felt that they were uncaring, cold, and ignorant people. For a long time, I thought of them as if they were guilty of some horrible crime.

I know I was judged by them as well, and for many years there was little to no contact between us. One day I woke up and realized that I accepted who I was and who I had become. With that awareness, it no longer mattered what they thought of me.

I then realized that perhaps I was judging them in a way that kept them from knowing me. So I stopped, stood back, and listened to them. I learned who they were and allowed them—as they were—back into my life. I have now released all past judgments about them. I no longer feel the way I once did about who they were or who I was, because I now know they're not the same people they were then, and neither am I. Once I dropped my assessment of them, I discovered that I like them and they like me.

I also judged men very negatively. I'd been so hurt by almost every man I'd had contact with from the age of five that I really felt there were no good men on this earth—that they were all mean, hurtful beings. I kept that feeling well into my 20s, at times abusing myself with my choices, until I realized that not all of them were the same. Some men are wonderful, kind, thoughtful people. I then changed the way I saw them; and from that moment on, I began to create wonderful, healthy relationships with men from all races, ages, and beliefs. Since releasing my negative, self-limiting condemnation of men I've found a wonderful partner. He loves, respects, and treats me as I treat him—with acceptance.

I judged women poorly as well. I had such a low self-image that any woman who was beautiful, thin, or intelligent was a bitch to me. There was no tolerance for those who were taller than I am, because in my past, I felt that tall women were more deserving than I was. I evaluated them based on how my ego was trained. I believed it when I was told that I'd never amount to much because I was too short to be anything worthwhile. As a result, I hated women and girls who were taller. I now look upon them as my equals—and no, I didn't gain any extra inches, but I sure did grow to accept them when I stopped judging them as better than I am.

I was told as a child that I was a dog, and in my first relationship my partner called me similar names—and I believed it all. I thought that I was a very unattractive person; I looked into the mirror and I saw that dog. I judged my appearance based on what I was told growing up. One day I was at my son's baseball game, and a complete *stranger—a very pretty, kind woman—started talking to me. She complimented my hair, my eyes, and my overall appearance. She told me that I emitted a beautiful light of peace from my image. This was the first time I'd heard such kind words about how I looked, and I was moved. I went home that evening and could see what she saw. From that moment on, I no longer judged my appearance based on my ego. I decided to control that negative, self-limiting inner dialogue, and now I know that I'm a beautiful woman.*

I accepted that I've judged and that I was judged. I now accept that such behavior keeps me from seeing the truth. Now I ask myself: Whom do I judge? *If I catch myself not being accepting of others, I stop myself and ask myself:* Why? Is this old training coming back, or is there something here for me to pay attention to and/or learn from? *I no longer condemn; I analyze without ego's control.*

My intention for this letter is to become more accepting of my true self without ego's control. With that intention in mind—and with the full awareness of whom I've judged and why—I once again ask myself: Who am I without ego's control? Who do I want to be? What do I want out of this lifetime?

I'm a complete person who loves herself and accepts her gifts, her faults, and her past. I see myself through my true eyes. I acknowledge that I'm not without flaws, and I accept all of me for who I truly am. I'm able to look in the mirror and see the person I've become, and I'm proud of her.

I also accept who I can become and understand that the path ahead of me is mine to create. I accept that I'm able to create any outcome I desire. I'm able to tolerate change and move on in that direction without fear. I've made peace with the fact that the journey ahead of me may not be easy at all times, and I now know that I'm capable of changing my path and creating better results for myself.

I accept that the perceptions others have of me no longer control how my ego manipulates my thoughts. I'm a strong person—capable of love, honesty, and a peaceful life without ego's control. I affirm that I want to be the best teacher I can be. I know that the past is over, and I am able to embrace all that was. It can no longer affect me in a negative way unless I allow it to do so. I accept that for the rest of this life, I will serve my true purpose and live as my authentic self, free from others' judgments.

I now accept others because I know that judgment is a self-reflection that creates negative outcomes. I'm free to love myself; and I'm free of my negative, self-limiting thoughts. I accept that I'm better than I allowed myself to believe I was.

In all that was, I've learned; and in all that will be, I will learn. I acknowledge that there will be more for me to learn and experience, and I embrace the future. I accept my true self; my truth; and that I'm capable of being loved for me, not for who I create myself to be.

CHAPTER THREE

THE KEY OF FORGIVENESS

USE THE KEY OF FORGIVENESS
TO FREE YOURSELF FROM THE PAST

> *I cannot go back and change the past.*
> *I accept that those experiences were simply*
> *lessons from which I have learned.*

In order to maintain privacy after using a shared computer, you can quickly and easily push a few buttons and clear the history of your Internet surfing—essentially, you can erase the past. What if you could do the same thing to *your* past—hit a button and "clear the history" of your life? Wouldn't it be wonderful if you could magically delete any part of it that created guilt, sadness, regret, or pain? Well, no, it really wouldn't. It's a good thing you can't actually do that, or you'd end up losing some of the most valuable lessons you've ever learned.

Your life experiences—from the unbelievably joyous to the gut-wrenchingly painful—serve you in tremendous ways. They can help you create the best *you* that you can be and the best *life* you can possibly live. You don't have to delete experiences; you just need to clear negative feelings, save positive lessons, and create desired outcomes. How? Use the key of forgiveness.

What is forgiveness? It's understanding that you can't go back and change the past. It's accepting that those experiences—no matter how traumatic, painful, or unhappy they may have been—were simply lessons from which to learn. On all levels—whether negative or positive, emotional, physical, psychological, or spiritual—those lessons were meant to teach you how to be yourself in this moment. You need to understand and accept that today you're the person you are because of what you've learned. Once you accept those lessons— *and truly learn from them*—the negatives of yesterday will never affect you again. You won't carry doubt, fear, and guilt. Instead, you'll be free.

Forgiveness is one of the best gifts you can give yourself. Until you have it within yourself, you remain stuck. You become stagnant in every opportunity. However, with forgiveness, you no longer hold back and defeat yourself. You're free to move on, to close the door on any negatives of the past. Tomorrow, anything that comes with you will only be positive. You'll only take with you what will serve your future—what will help you fulfill your purpose. You'll be free to evolve into the next higher level of self. You'll be able to truly love yourself.

In order to do this, you first need to become aware of *who* it is you need to forgive: everyone! This includes everybody whom you've thought of negatively because of something they said or did. This also applies to your neighbors, your parents, the kids who bullied you in school, the boss who fired you, the spouse who hurt you, and the friend who lied to you.

You also need to forgive yourself. It's okay that your mind believed the things it did and that you held yourself in negative patterns (such as choosing a partner who's an abuser, an alcoholic, a workaholic, or someone who's unloving and never there). You have to forgive your ego and your spirit for not taking control sooner. Do this in all aspects of life.

This key will give you the ability to forgive *yourself* for everything you believe you've done wrong as well as forgive *others* who've contributed to any anxieties and traumas in your past. It will help you free yourself and release negativity. It will enable you to look back on every life situation without pain, guilt, sadness, regret, resentment, anger, doubt, blame, or remorse. It's time to use this third key in your own life. Begin with self-forgiveness.

I'm free to forgive myself and others.

FORGIVE YOURSELF FOR ERRORS OF THE PAST

I accept that although I've made errors in the past, I release them and make new choices today that allow me to create a positive future. I no longer negatively judge myself. I give myself love, forgiveness, and understanding.

In his book *For One More Day,* Mitch Albom writes: "I met a man once who did a lot of mountain climbing. I asked him which was harder, ascending or descending? He said without a doubt descending, because when ascending, you were so focused on reaching the top, you avoided mistakes. 'The backside of a mountain is a fight against human nature,' he said. 'You have to care as much about yourself on the way down as you did on the way up.'" That's good advice to remember.

It's easy to value, accept, and care about yourself "on the way up," when you're on track to achieving your dreams, everything is going well, and you're doing the right things. Yet "on the way down"—when you've made a mistake, veered off course, or have found yourself regretting the choices you've made . . . self-worth, self-approval, and self-love may be the first to be discarded. During those times, you may believe that you don't deserve to carry these tools on your journey and that you're unworthy, undeserving, and unlovable. But that's just a trick of the ego.

The truth is that you came into this world worthy, deserving, and lovable; and *no matter what has happened since,* you're just as worthy, deserving, and lovable in this very moment as you were on the day you were born. You're still that same perfect being. You've learned things; that's the only difference. Yes, sometimes your lessons may have been negative, judgmental, fearful, and worrisome. You may have made some mistakes.

On the other hand, maybe they weren't actually "mistakes." Perhaps you needed to make those choices in order to learn everything you did. Either way, what's happened in the past is over; it's finished. It's time for you to forgive yourself. For everything you *believe* you've done wrong—not giving love when someone needed it, not being supportive, creating negative energy in another person's life or in your own, not being honorable or respectable—forgive yourself and allow yourself to move forward.

I accept that in each experience lies the opportunity for me to learn valuable lessons.

You, just like everyone else, are here to journey on your own individual and unique path. You're here to learn and to absorb information. Along your journey, you may have made some errors and done some things you're not proud of—everybody has. Understand that it's okay for you to have experienced those things. Some of them were necessary in order for you to fulfill your life purposes. If they hadn't occurred, you wouldn't have the knowledge that will allow you to create the best possible you and the best possible tomorrow.

Take all of your experiences and become empowered by them. You can't change them, but you can discover something of value in them. When you do so, you'll be able to extend forgiveness to yourself and others. By choosing to learn the lesson completely in the present, you'll enable yourself to move forward and stop negative cycles from repeating. Begin by asking yourself: *What have I truly learned about myself, and with what lesson am I moving forward?*

I ask myself daily: "What have I learned?"

Take the time to genuinely discover the answers. Perhaps you made an error in judgment, but it taught you to set boundaries. Maybe you made a poor choice but learned what to *start* doing or what to *stop*. These are very valuable lessons. Perhaps the experience showed you what you will or will not allow and accept into your life. Maybe you decided to stop judging others for their choices; through your experience you discovered acceptance. This can be a huge blessing.

Release any negative feelings by telling yourself: *Okay, I made a mistake. The error has taught me that if I act or react in that way, or if I allow that into my life, this is how it will affect me.* Accept the situation as an experience you've had, and then forgive yourself by knowing that you've gained wisdom from it. Celebrate that accomplishment; it's significant!

You must take the time to learn the lessons *completely,* however, otherwise you'll keep repeating negative patterns and creating the same roadblocks. Say, for instance, somebody told you that you're a negative and judgmental person. After the verbal exchange, you said to yourself: *I don't like that person anymore because of what she said to me.* If you decide that you need to understand that you can sometimes be seen as negative and judgmental, it was a lesson learned. If, instead, you choose to be offended and never talk to that person again, you haven't grown. You've avoided the lesson. Therefore, it's necessary to repeat the experience so that you have the opportunity to learn what you were meant to.

You'll create the same experiences over and over again until you realize: *Oh, wait a minute. I'm on the same path. I remember hearing this about myself from others before. I understand what she's telling me. She's saying that she witnesses negative and judgmental tendencies in me. That's not a positive part of my personality, and it doesn't serve me or others. I'm going to learn from that and try to change. I'll choose to become less judgmental, more open, and more understanding. I decide to learn that lesson now, complete it, and move on to the next level.* Once the lesson is learned, you don't have to repeat it again. Forgive yourself for not learning it sooner and move on.

I now view myself based on "what is," not "what was."

An additional step in helping you forgive yourself is to judge yourself based on today instead of the past. What are you doing right now? You're reading this book. You're doing the work necessary to evolve to the next level, to find out who you are without ego, to accept yourself and release all negative judgments, and to forgive yourself and free yourself from the past. Judge yourself in accordance with that because it's amazing. It's commendable and honorable. That means—based on what *is*—you're good, commendable, and honorable. You can feel good.

It's okay that the past happened, but that's what *was*. Now focus on the present, and change yourself and your life based on the lessons you've learned from it. If where you are and who you are don't match what you want, then be more and create more. Make new choices, think new thoughts, take new actions, and free yourself from perceived limitations. Before you know it, you and your life will begin to unfold in significant and magnificent ways. Start in this moment by asking yourself: *What is it that I really want for my life? Who am I really? Who is it that I want to become?* You're capable of creating a new experience for yourself.

> *I accept that I'm capable of change.*
> *I'm strong, and I deserve a new start.*

Another step toward forgiving yourself is accepting that you're capable of *change.* You really are. Yes, it may be true that a tiger never changes its stripes and a leopard never changes its spots; but here's a newsflash: you're not a tiger or a leopard. You're human, and you're very capable of transforming your life. Anytime you choose, you can re-create yourself—and it all starts now.

The power to create the best *you* and the best *life* possible for tomorrow is in this moment. You *can* find the strength within to use the key of forgiveness to let go of the past and move into the future with a new perspective and an abundant appreciation for this fresh start. You have the opportunity to create an outcome for your life that's of *your* choosing.

This is true no matter what your current situation. Say, for instance, you're aware that you're an alcoholic, a drug addict, a compulsive gambler, or an abusive person, but you've decided that you don't want that. Forgive yourself by accepting that you're capable of making changes, and then take control. Use the power of your mind to say: *I'm strong. I do deserve a new start. It's okay to be me. It's okay to have had my experiences. I accept that this is how I've lived, and I'm aware of how it has affected me. I forgive myself now for living that life, and I choose to never go back to it. I will break the patterns and cycles of the past.*

You're not letting yourself off the hook and telling yourself that it's okay to be an alcoholic, a drug addict, a compulsive gambler, or an abusive person. You're not giving yourself permission to do any of that again, believing it doesn't matter. What you *are* doing is letting yourself know that the past is over and it's okay for you to have experienced what you did because you learned your lesson. Now that it's completely understood, you're never going back there again. You're not going to repeat these patterns. You've changed, and it's okay to move on.

You can be happy with yourself. You can enjoy peace because you choose to no longer be controlled by your ego. It's okay to be you. It's good to love and forgive yourself for everything that *was* and start living for tomorrow. Create the destiny that you truly know you're capable of.

You *can* become the person you want to be. You *can* change—if you do the work. Even if you've been very negative and hurtful, you can choose to transform and not be like that any longer. You can become a committed, honest, loving, compassionate individual; you never have to go back and re-create negativity in your life or the lives of others. Tell yourself: *I no longer live in that mind-set. I no longer think those thoughts. I'm no longer controlled by my ego's presence.*

I forgive myself for negative choices of the past by living in honesty today. I now choose to live in truth.

What does it mean to live in truth? It means to live honestly at all levels. It's not just about what you say; it's also about thoughts, actions, and the way you live. This involves authenticity—to live in alignment with who you know your true self to be. What you'll receive is very empowering. You become free to live and explore the truth of who you really are as you move toward the future. You're at liberty to change, develop, and go further in your own life within your own true spirit and mind.

Maybe you're aware that up until now you haven't had a very honest life. Perhaps at one time you lied, stole, or cheated. It's okay, because that's who you were *then,* not who you are *now.* You've changed. You've taken the steps to become aware of who you really are, you've discovered how to accept yourself on a new level, and you've released harmful judgments against yourself and others. Those negative patterns that once controlled your life, your work, your relationships—they're all in the past. They're over. Today, choose to live in honesty.

To create a truthful life, you need to be honest with yourself and with others in each and every moment. Imagine, for instance, that you're standing in a room and the person beside you gets blamed for something you've done. You need to confess that it was you. Speak up in that moment, not after the time has passed. Honesty doesn't come from talking to the wrongly accused at a later date and saying, "I'm really sorry. I should have said something." It needs to be in the moment the other person was blamed for something you did.

That being said, there may be some things you've said or done in the past for which you'd like to apologize. If your expression of regret will help and heal another person, by all means proceed. However, be careful! If telling the truth, confessing, or asking for forgiveness is going to devastate other people or destroy their lives, then stop. Don't let your ego manipulate you into thinking that you *need* to talk to them and tell them everything. Confess to yourself, learn the lesson, forgive yourself, and move on. Making a private inner confession is also best if bringing up a past experience could simply create turmoil in someone else's life. Sometimes when you ask for forgiveness from people who aren't ready, it can cause more disruption and chaos.

In these situations, it's best to write a letter of forgiveness to yourself. In it, note all the things for which you believe you need to be forgiven but are best left unsaid in order to protect someone else. You might write down: *I lied to a friend and I never told her the truth. I chose not to tell her the truth because I knew it would hurt her. At the time she wasn't ready. I've carried this burden, but I'm asking for forgiveness. Confessing to her today wouldn't change the situation and would cause her pain. I've chosen to forgive myself for that lie, and I can move on knowing that it was best to protect her.* Forgive yourself. By doing so, you're no longer manipulated by the past.

> *I choose to release guilt because*
> *I'm aware that it's an engine for my ego.*

You have to realize that when it comes to forgiveness—true forgiveness and having a forgiving mindset—you'll sometimes carry guilt. Suppose, for example, you've made a mistake and you say to yourself: *I've done something wrong, and I'm choosing to seek forgiveness from myself because I know that it won't serve anyone if I confess and ask for others to absolve me.* Yet sometimes you feel guilty for what's occurred.

Guilt is one of the engines of the ego. That's why a lot of people return to the same negative patterns and *re*-create the same chaos in their lives. Even after they've done the work, years later they're still making the same choices and still feeling the same way because they still carry the guilt.

You have to let go of the shame that's related to what happened yesterday because it's harmful to your well-being. You must abandon it in order to evolve and reach the next level of your inner self. The only way for you to be truly free and beyond ego's control is to release the guilt. You can't have liberty until you let go of the past.

To release guilt, you need to completely learn the lesson and forgive yourself for how you got to where you are now. Some wisdom comes through positive experiences and some through negative ones. In either case, as long as you truly learn the lesson completely, it was worth what happened, so there's no need to judge yourself. If you're judging yourself based on how you've come to grips with situations in your personal history, switch your thinking around and instead base it on how you're going to learn tomorrow, in the future. This shift in your viewpoint empowers you to make changes and take charge of your life. Now your ego is no longer in control of judgment—*you* are.

Reflect on a time in your life when you know that you experienced something that was wrong. It was deceptive, dishonest, hateful, hurtful, or cruel. Are you still carrying the emotional baggage of guilt from that experience? Release it. Allow your heart and spirit to know it: *Yes, I've gone through this experience, and I understand why I feel the guilt.*

Next, ask yourself: *What is it that I was meant to learn?* You have to examine the event and what you took away from it. You know deep within what the lessons are. When you learn and understand, you're able to release the guilt and the emotional attachment to it.

I now free myself from the
self-limiting guilt I've been carrying.

Suppose, for instance, you're feeling guilty about not being honest to somebody decades ago, which ultimately ruined your friendship. What did you learn? Perhaps you recognized the pain that deception causes; maybe you discovered how valuable and rare friendships are; or it could be that you found out how much dishonesty can hurt and destroy, and how honesty can heal and mend. If you learned the lesson fully, you won't repeat the behavior. You can accept that and free yourself from the guilt. You'll no longer feel saddened or empty because of the experience. You've served that purpose, and now it's over and complete. On the other hand, if you *don't* get the message, it's not valuable to you and you'll continue to carry guilt.

It's important to make sure you learn a *positive* lesson that will serve you and help you to live honestly and truthfully. For instance, if someone stole something from a store and is arrested for shoplifting, it won't serve him if he decides it's important to avoid getting caught. If that's what he takes from the experience, it's because he's living under ego's control. A positive lesson would be to stop stealing, or maybe he needs to seek help. Perhaps he has a disorder such as kleptomania, and he needs help to heal and correct it. It could be that he must learn remorse. Maybe he's been a crime victim and he needs to learn to understand the psychological mind. Unless this person looks at what wisdom can be gained, he'll continue to repeat the same patterns.

Take the time to discover the positive lesson in the experience and then affirm to yourself: *I allow myself forgiveness for what I have done. I release the guilt related to it because I have learned the lesson and it is complete. I have freedom from that experience to live without that part of my past holding me back. I no longer repeat that behavior. I choose instead to walk a straight path and continue to motivate myself with positive and loving thoughts.*

It's time to close the door to yesterday and open your life to positive forward motion today. Forgive yourself, release the guilt, and allow self-worth, self-respect, and self-love to flow into your life. Do this by acknowledging that you can't go back and change history and by accepting that those experiences have taught you many precious lessons. There are incredible mountains yet to climb and many more things to learn. On your journey, always remember to care as much about yourself on the way down as you did on the way up—you really do deserve it!

FORGIVE OTHERS FOR ERRORS OF THEIR EGOS

I'm aware that some issues of my past have contributed to who I am today. Not all parts of my path have created a positive me. I'm capable of changing how I view the negative aspects of what's gone before. I'm capable of using my memories to change how I react today, processing information without ego's control.

You can't go back and alter anything that occurred yesterday, but you can learn to accept the past and forgive others for the part they played in your experiences. It's crucial for you to do the work and forgive everyone because harboring anger, resentment, or blame hurts *you* more than anyone else.

In forgiving others, it's important to realize that you're not condoning poor behavior. You simply understand that you can't change what's happened, and you accept that there are lessons for you to learn in those experiences. You don't have to necessarily like *how* you came to be where you are today, but you can come to a place where you're grateful because you're stronger. Those situations make you tougher, more aware, more conscious, and more capable. You can treasure the fact that you've learned so very much. In this state of gratitude, your ego can't use memories to control or defeat any part of you.

How can you get to that place of gratitude when you're dealing with extremely painful events? How can you be thankful if an experience hurt so much that it still affects you today, perhaps because you associate certain things in your life with the memory? Maybe you have intimacy or commitment issues, eating disorders, or low self-esteem because of those associations. How can you forgive others for what's happened when you're still coping with residual issues and pain today? You arrive at a place of gratitude by looking back on your memories, discovering where they began, processing them without ego's control, and learning the lesson completely.

The following pages will help you do that. You're about to take a journey into your past and learn how to forgive everyone who contributed to your experiences and the lessons you learned between birth and the present day.

From Birth to Age 4

As outlined in the first chapter, you may not have a memory of anything that happened during this block of time. Your subconscious mind, however, is storing information. For example, imagine that the second you're born, the doctor exclaims, "Big baby!" Those first words are programmed into the mind. In addition, suppose that from birth, your mother—who has an obesity problem herself—feeds you sugar-sweetened applesauce with your baby formula. She gives you cookies and candy once you can eat solid food. Now you're three years old and you already weigh 70 pounds. You're big, just like the doctor said. Then you're four years old, you're still big, and you're starting to feel the emotions related to being an overweight child. The kids around you are little. You're taller, heavier, and maybe stronger than they are; perhaps you're a bully because of it. Unfortunately, that's how you were programmed; that's what you were taught. As an adult, you may still be struggling with eating issues and low self-esteem.

I'm capable of taking control of my negative habits.

You might begin blaming others, asking: "Why didn't you tell me during those formative years that I was a good child—smart, and capable of becoming anything I wanted to become? Why didn't you tell me that I had the right to be myself? Why didn't you give me the nutrition, understanding, honesty, and love that I needed without conditions and judgments?"

The answer to those questions is quite possibly that the individuals who surrounded you had similar experiences in their own pasts. They didn't have the keys of awareness, acceptance, or forgiveness. They were projecting their own egos upon you because they, too, were being controlled and manipulated. They were simply passing on their own perceptions and beliefs.

What we know is what we teach others. If the authority figures in your life haven't become aware of who they truly are and accepted and forgiven themselves, the pattern continues. It's up to you to break the cycle. This is where forgiveness comes in. You need to forgive yourself, others, and the past. Forgive your mom, the doctor, and so on. Don't blame them; they weren't aware.

You also have to forgive yourself for not knowing who you truly were. Accept that during this period of time, you were programmed based on other people's perceptions of you. What others believed about you is not your true identity; it's not your inner self. It was only their egos that projected it upon you. At that time, you were incapable of saying: "This isn't who I really am. I'm healthy. I'm smart. I'm tall. I can achieve all that I desire." You didn't have the keys—now you do.

I am now my true self, unlimited by others' perceptions.

When you go back and analyze the events in your life, you might become aware that you have an abandonment issue. Maybe you have fear because you were left alone. Perhaps your babysitter was abusive and mean and yelled at you—so now you're afraid of confrontation. Forgive that period of your life. Recognize that your anxieties are only based on past programming. Choose to let your mind, spirit, and heart be free from emotional barriers and the imbalances they've caused. Let yourself be free, and allow your spirit to move on from that time in your past.

I have released all blame that I once cast upon others. I accept the lessons I learned. I understand that I'm capable of using them to help myself achieve my true identity.

When you feel there's something about you that's not 100 percent positive, don't blame it on anyone else. Use the key of forgiveness to free others and yourself from those negative cycles. When you do so, you've changed the patterns and the programming of your mind. You're now capable of accepting that that period of time was very valuable because of the lessons you've learned. It was necessary for you to have those experiences in order to fulfill the themes related to your true purpose. Now that process is complete. You've learned from what happened; it's over and you're moving on.

You can say to yourself: *I've gone through the first stage of my life and understand that's where my programming came from. I'm now okay with that; I understand why part of my personality may not be exactly as I want it to be. I accept myself.* Be aware that your ego will try to take control of this self-discovery and tell you: *You can't let go of that.* So, you must fight back and say, *Oh yes, I can!* Anytime you have a memory of the past that's negative and makes you feel less than your true self, let ego know that you're 100 percent capable of becoming the person you dream of being and that you won't allow that judgmental, angry, and controlling mind to take over.

Affirm to yourself that you're back in control—the person you were born to be, not the identity that was created by society. As you work through this next stage of life, make a conscious effort to think positively. That's how you let go, move on, and progress to the next level of life.

I'm now aware of how capable I am.

Ages 4 to 10

As described in Chapter 1, these are the "experience" years. You're trying new things and you're learning. Your mind is absorbing everything, and you're very open to new information. There's so much that you're readily taking in. Now you're responsible as well, because you've gained independence. You're off on your own, playing in the backyard. Your mom doesn't need to be right beside you anymore. Someone's watching you from the back window, but you have independence and you're learning things based on what you want to experience.

You decide that you want to know what it's like to go over the fence, so that's what you do. You discover that on the other side there's a big dog, and it bites you. You've just had a traumatic experience. It's unhappy and painful. You're in the hospital, bleeding, and you'll have scars for life. Are you going to blame the dog? Are you going to stay angry with the dog's owner? The fact is that *you* chose to climb over the fence. Forgive yourself for doing so, forgive the dog, and forgive its owner by learning from the experience.

What did you discover? Well, those scars have taught you to never do that again and to pay attention to the fact that you're protected within the bounds of your property. It's a boundary that you can push outward, but you have to be careful about what's on the other side. Although you know that you're strong and capable, that you want to learn, and that you want to experience new things, you also have to be aware. Those are valuable lessons.

Another way of looking at this example in terms of forgiveness is to see the dog as having taught you a lesson. Forgive the animal because you *did* ask for it to come into your life. If that wasn't so, then why is it that another child climbed over the fence and didn't get bitten by the dog—but you did? It's because you needed it; learn the lesson so that it's complete and so you don't have to repeat it in the future.

Continue to find the positive in every experience and to forgive. From four to ten years of age, you're learning from all kinds of things. Positive or negative, it's all being stored in your mind, and your perceptions are being formed. Some of these can create fear and anxiety; others can create physical, mental, emotional, or psychological disorders—all based on how you filter the experience.

For instance, imagine you were seven years old and in the second grade when the teacher reprimanded you and gave you a slap on the hand in front of your whole class. You were embarrassed by it. You felt weakened and you became withdrawn. Maybe that wasn't what you were supposed to have taken with you from that day. Perhaps you should have learned to be a powerful leader in the classroom so that other people saw that you were a good student and followed your example. Maybe that run-in was meant to help you start becoming the leader you were born to be. In every chapter of life, take the positive lessons with you.

Admittedly, this can be more challenging to do when the experiences are very traumatic, such as being assaulted. This sort of event programs pain into your ego. Whether the anguish is physical, emotional, mental, or psychological in nature, the lessons you take from it will ultimately carve out whether you're going to be loving toward yourself—choosing self-awareness, acceptance, and forgiveness—or whether you're going to be angry as an adult and hurtful toward yourself and others.

*I forgive myself for having allowed
negative thoughts to control my outcome.*

How do you choose the former, extending love toward yourself and choosing to forgive when something so painful has happened? You proceed in the same way you do with every other experience: you accept that you can't go back and change what's occurred, but acknowledge that you can learn valuable lessons from it. Maybe the message was to ask for protection or to be more aware of your surroundings. Perhaps you discovered a desire to protect others, and as a result find yourself working in a career that's allowing you to fulfill your purpose. When you know that everything builds on the theme of your life, serving that purpose, then you can forgive anything in that period of time—be it negative or positive.

Learn any and every lesson that will empower you. You deserve to be strong. You don't need to carry the negative association of this experience until your death. You are worthy of peace, joy, and happiness. Do everything you can to find ways to take positive lessons from every experience. Since you can't go back and change it, shift your perception. Suck all of the goodness out of it that you can.

Have you had tough experiences that left emotional, physical, or psychological scars? If so, are you going to allow those scars to keep you from evolving, developing, becoming strong, or realizing your true identity? You don't have to. You can systematically heal yourself. Don't look at the scars every single day and tell yourself that they're there because you did something wrong, you made a mistake, or you were a bad person. That's just your ego talking. Don't listen, or you'll believe it to be true and the scar won't heal.

Instead, look at the scar and say, *Yes—that was tough. That was a hard thing to go through. Although it was extremely painful, it was a valuable experience in my life, and it will never be repeated again. The scar may be ugly right now, but I'm going to allow it to heal. I'll watch it as it begins to mend, releasing the negative emotional attachment to it. I'm going to be okay. I won't cover and hide it. Instead, I'm going to expose it completely. I'm going to let my mind, body, and spirit feel it so that I can become totally conscious of who I am and what I've learned. I'm finished with this experience, and I'll no longer allow it to negatively affect me.*

You *are* finished with it. It's in past; it's over. Take the positive lessons forward with you because they give you strength. However, free yourself of anything that's negative. Become aware that you no longer need to hold on to this painful memory. Accept it, forgive others, and move yourself through it. The memory will remain someplace inside your mind, and if you choose to retrieve it and reanalyze it, you can. However, you'll no longer associate negative feelings with it because the lessons are yours now. You've chosen your own freedom, and you don't have to carry the past with you. It's over and done, and you're stronger because of it.

During these years, you can also be programmed by the people who are positive influences. Maybe your dad was a doctor, nurse, or telephone repairman and you decided that you were going to be that, too, when you grew up. You wanted to be just like your dad: good, kind, loving, honest, and giving. Perhaps that's what your parents taught you to be because they learned how to function without judgment and without ego.

It's important to understand that as wonderful as *positive* messages feel, too many of them can be imbalanced. Say, for instance, you're told every day: "You're a princess. You're just so beautiful." You're between the ages of four and ten, and you haven't yet grown, developed, or matured in any way. Time passes, and you're 12 years old. All of a sudden puberty kicks in. You're a little bit heavy, and your adult teeth grow in a little crooked. Maybe your hair is really thin, and you envy your friend who has beautiful, thick hair. You want to look the way she does because your ego tells you that *she* looks like a princess and you don't. You feel terrible about yourself because you've been told that you're a princess and you want to be that ideal. You think you need to be the smartest and best-looking girl in order to be accepted and loved, but you don't feel that way. You don't understand who your authentic self is yet.

Then you become an adult and loathe yourself because you're not a princess. You must forgive your parents for how they contributed to the way you feel about yourself today by accepting that even in an experience of too much positive reinforcement there are wonderful things to be learned. Figure out what you've gained in every experience so that you can complete the lesson and free yourself from the imbalances.

I'm capable of accepting all lessons
in whatever form they come.

Ages 10 to 20

Between the ages of 10 and 20, you've been programmed to believe who you are. Say, for instance, you're 12 years old and you ask your mom if you can help her cook dinner. She refuses and says you don't know how to do it right—you'll just be in her way. Your ego grabs hold of that situation and tells you that you're worth nothing to her. You're just a bother. Well, maybe your mom only said that because she was tired, or perhaps her mom treated her the same way. Who knows? Whatever the reason, you were just programmed to believe that you're worthless, a bother, and in the way.

What if you'd asked to help that night because part of your life purpose was to become a chef? That response could cause you to veer off course when your ego uses it to fill your mind with negative beliefs about yourself. Your ego tells you that you're not going to be a chef because you don't know how to cook right, and you just get in the way in the kitchen. You believe what you're thinking. It must be the truth because you're only 12 years old and your mom said so herself. Your mom knows everything.

Now you're 25, 30, or 40 years old, and you're looking back at that episode, feeling angry with your mother for saying those things. You've used the awareness key to realize that you've always wanted to be a chef but that experience prevented you from reaching your goal. It's okay; it's not too late. You can still become a chef. In the meantime, you've got to forgive your mom's participation in your ego's creation. Learn from the experience and move on.

From that experience, perhaps other lessons followed. Maybe that night your dad heard what your mom said and he interjected, "Hey, wait! I want our son to help you cook dinner tonight because I think he might be really good." Maybe your dad was supportive. He knew that you shouldn't limit a child, but instead should say: "Yes, you can!" Perhaps dinner was delicious that night. Now you're 45 and a fantastic chef. In essence, the experience with your mom had a part in achieving your purpose, so forgive her. Otherwise, the anxiety can affect what you're doing today. For instance, if you had to appear on a television show about being a top chef and you hadn't forgiven your mother, she'll still be in the back of your mind saying: *You're not good. You can't do it right. Get out of the kitchen.* Forgive her, forgive the experience, and let go of ego's control.

It really is between the ages of 10 and 20 when you learn to let ego control you. Let's say that you're 16 and at your first job. Somebody tells you that you're incompetent and you don't know anything. Well, you've never worked before, and now you feel terrible. That comment can become a self-fulfilling prophecy. You're so afraid of being criticized again that you doubt yourself and are fearful. Because you don't learn as well when you're anxious and fearful, you end up making more mistakes.

Experiences like that, especially when you're in this age range, stick with you. Consider this next scenario: You're approaching your late teens and are graduating from high school. You didn't have the best marks, but you passed. You're proud of yourself. You get up, cross the stage, and receive your diploma; that night you go out and have a grand old time. The next week, you're sitting in the living room when your dad says, "You could have done better. I sure hope things improve when you go to college." All that pride in your accomplishment vanishes.

Now you're on your way to college and worrying about not getting great marks there. Your dad pointed out that you didn't do very well in the past, so you believe you're not that good. Without the keys of awareness, acceptance, and forgiveness, those programmed beliefs could negatively affect your studies and ultimately affect the course of your life.

I now hold the keys of awareness, acceptance, and forgiveness. I'm ready to move to my freedom.

On the other hand, suppose you're sitting in the living room with your dad and he says, "You're going off to college this year, and I'm really proud of you. I know you're going to do a really great job. You've

111

obviously done well in high school, and you're a good person. I know that anything you want in this lifetime is possible. Tomorrow, I want you to wake up and remind yourself of that. I also want you to know that no matter where you are in the world, as long as you're being yourself and you're being honest, you're going to succeed at whatever it is you desire."

Many parents do tell their kids these kinds of things. Often, they consciously tell their children they want them to be their best and to do everything they need to do to follow their dreams. That's a good gift to give as a parent. If that was the experience you had, you're going to go to college and succeed. You're going to excel and enjoy it. You'll have the motivation to know you can do anything. That's a positive ego balance.

Looking back, what things were difficult for you between the ages of 10 and 20? What experiences caused you to be very fearful of becoming who and what you truly desire? What events caused you to be incapable of loving yourself? If you allow your ego to take control based on what occurred during that time, you'll never get beyond it. But if you allow for change and forgive those traumatic events, you can then carve out a new path for your own future. You're no longer living in self-doubt or feel as if you're incapable. You're allowing yourself to move forward and become that great student.

Maybe you're 47 years old now and you want to go back to school because you didn't do well the first time. That was back when the old self wasn't aware. You were judgmental and fearful. Now, however, you can do anything. That's right! There are no limitations, no boundaries. You're going to go back to college, and you're going to do really well this time. You've still got 20 years left to work, and you want to be a doctor. Can you do it? Of course you can. If you've taken advantage of self-forgiveness, there's nothing that can hold you back. Begin to move forward and fulfill the purpose of your life.

> *I allow for forgiveness today, and I've*
> *made the decision to live my purpose.*

When you're aware of the issues your ego's negative programming has created, you can forgive everyone and live the rest of your life based on your decision to live your purpose. You can go out and become a lawyer if that's what you want to do. Maybe you're going to choose a type of law that helps children become empowered and free. Perhaps you want to teach people how to reflect on the past stages of their lives and understand how each stage affects their development, as you've just done here. You may want everyone to understand that, like you, they can succeed—no boundaries, no limitations.

So you wanted to be a lawyer but when you were eight years old, your dad said, "You're too dumb and lazy. Stop dreaming because you're not going to amount to anything. You're no good to anybody." Now you've forgiven him. You say to yourself: *Dad, it's okay that you didn't believe in me, because I believe in me. I know the "me" that you never did, and I'm proud. I understand myself, and I'm okay. I've forgiven you for not understanding yourself and for being judgmental. I've forgiven you for saying the things you did because you probably had someone say them to you, and you've never freed yourself. You haven't allowed yourself to move on and evolve to a higher level of self. I forgive you, and it feels good.*

Now anything is possible. You don't have the barriers, the weights, and the past that was keeping you from being yourself. The rest of your life is based on what you make it. Today, prepare for tomorrow, knowing that it will be filled with the hopes, dreams, and aspirations you've always had.

I know I can be in total control over my ego's perceptions.

As you're reading this, you might notice your ego saying: *No, you can't! Are you crazy? My God, have you lost your marbles? Who do you think you are?* Allow your true identity to reply: *Today, I'm going to make my dreams and aspirations come true because I'm capable. There's nothing that holds me back. I live in a position of freedom. I've forgiven. I know who I am, and I accept it. I've moved myself toward the freedom that's mine, and I create the rest of this path. I know what destiny is open to me. I'm going to serve my purpose. There's really nothing that holds me back. No matter what anyone else says, I know within myself that this is what I've chosen. It's my true purpose, and I'm capable.*

Does this mean that forevermore you'll be without lessons, pain, or the need to forgive yourself and others? No, and that's okay. Remember that your future experiences will benefit you, too; they'll continue to help you grow into the best person that you can be and to create the best life for yourself. During these times, once again use the key of forgiveness to overcome adversity, deal with imperfection, and to seize the chance to begin anew.

I realize I'm capable of surviving all future lessons.

SELF-REFLECTION: WHOM DO I NEED TO FORGIVE?

Today I'm aware and accept that I can't go back and change the past, and I realize that I'll find freedom in forgiveness. In this way, I become completely aware of the lessons I've learned. I'm a loving being and worthy of being freed from all that wasn't in service to my purpose.

You now have the key of forgiveness. You're aware of the fact that you can't go back and change the past, and you accept that you've learned some very valuable lessons from those experiences. It's time to apply this knowledge to your own life by writing another self-reflection letter—a letter of forgiveness.

Before you begin, take a few moments to affirm: *I allow my body, mind, and spirit to be forgiven of the past. I allow all my previous experiences to no longer be burdens. I'm worthy of more than I once realized. I release the judgments and forgive who I was. I'm becoming the self that's empowered and completely truthful. I know that honesty is real empowerment.*

The purpose of this self-reflection is twofold. First, you want to take the time for discovery. Look back on the past and ask yourself: *Whom do I need to forgive?*

Is it yourself? Is it your teachers, religion, friends, peers, or parents? What about your ego? Take the time and determine those you need to forgive.

The second purpose of this letter is to know who you were without forgiveness, who you are with it, and who you want to become with this key. For that reason, also use the letter to answer these three questions:

- Who was I *without* forgiveness?
- Who am I *with* forgiveness?
- Who do *I* want to be with forgiveness?

Begin your letter with the following declaration of intention:

*My intention for this letter is to identify whom
I need to forgive and to discover more deeply
who I was without forgiveness, who I am with
forgiveness, and who I want to be with forgiveness.*

Sample Letter of Forgiveness

Dear Self,

*My intention for this letter is to identify those
I need to forgive and to discover more deeply who*

I was without forgiveness, who I am with forgiveness, and who I want to be with forgiveness.

Who was I without forgiveness? I'm aware that before I forgave myself, I was always afraid to tell the truth. I was worried that if I was honest, others wouldn't like me. My ego took hold of that fear and controlled me to the point where I simply said the things everybody else wanted to hear. I'd tell them I was happy when I wasn't—that was a lie. I'd say that what they were doing was acceptable, even when it hurt me—another lie. I'd exaggerate who I was and pretend to be someone I wasn't—more lying. One lie after another, and my ego was in full control. It told me that I was a liar and therefore a bad person. It said I wasn't worthy of forgiveness, which made me lie even more. It was a vicious cycle.

The lack of forgiveness also made me feel guilty. I felt horrible because of the mistakes I'd made in the past. That made me feel even more unlovable and unacceptable. I tried to kill the pain with alcohol and food—but it didn't work. It just made the pain grow and made me drink and eat even more, which affected my physical well-being and appearance. I didn't like how I looked, and that made me feel even more unlovable. It also made me more afraid—which made me lie even more to others and myself. It was another negative loop that I couldn't get out of until I learned to forgive myself. And I did learn.

I forgive myself for lying to people to gain their love. I forgive myself for lying to myself over and over again. I forgive myself for not taking the time sooner to truly know who I am and to figure out what I truly want. I forgive myself for spending money I didn't have to impress others, for shrinking my inner light to please them, and for not knowing my worth. Because I didn't know how valuable I am, I gave pieces of myself away—beautiful, special pieces. I forgive myself for doing that. I also forgive myself for allowing people's opinions to stop me from doing what I truly wanted to do. With that forgiveness, I've just empowered myself to be capable of doing all of those things.

I forgive myself for drinking too much because it was only feeding my ego. I forgive my ego for making me a jealous and untrusting person and for keeping me in an internal prison throughout my entire life. I forgive myself for that past and all others who contributed to making my ego as strong as it was. I forgive those who ridiculed me or denied me love as a child. I forgive those who hurt me, lied to me, and judged me in a negative way—even when I knew I didn't deserve it. I realize I can't change what's happened, and I accept that I've learned many valuable lessons through those experiences.

Who am I with this forgiveness? I'm a strong, loving person who has been empowered by the many valuable lessons learned throughout my lifetime. One of the greatest was how much dishonesty hurts and destroys, and how much honesty heals and rebuilds. The Bible verse is right: The truth shall set you free. I understand that doesn't mean I confess all of my errors if doing so will create any negativity in another person's life. I accept that I can find forgiveness within my own heart. I know that I've learned the lessons and will never repeat those experiences again. They're over; they're in the past.

I also gained a deeper insight into myself. I discovered that I've carried guilt throughout my entire life because when I was a child, I wanted to be loved, yet I was denied affection at times by certain family members. Then when I grew older, I refused to give myself true, unconditional love. That's where the ego took hold; that's where the guilt came in. I carried the shame that I didn't allow myself to have the care that I needed. I always gave *myself to whomever would give me love. It didn't matter what kind it was. I'd take it—even though it really wasn't what I wanted.*

Yet today I'm honest with myself. I know what I want and what I will and won't accept. I'm happy with me; I love myself and the person I'm becoming. I respect that person.

I no longer judge myself in a negative way because I know that I needed to learn certain lessons. This knowledge serves me well as I walk the path that allows me to fulfill my purpose.

Therefore, the experiences of my past that weren't necessarily positive have definitely helped me shape a better life. No longer living those negative patterns allows me to have a more balanced and truthful experience, so I'm not judging myself based on who I was. I evaluate who I am and who I want to be. I create that in my mind and no longer allow negative perceptions of the past to manipulate or harness my abilities to focus on myself. I know I'm a better person because of the way I've shifted those patterns.

I forgive myself and others, and now the past is no longer able to manipulate me in any way. I'm not controlled by the way things were. I'm stronger because I'm more capable.

With forgiveness, I'm aware that I'm capable of honesty, and I'm now the person I've always wanted to be. I'm creating a truthful life that feels good in my spirit. I know that I can create a wonderful future without fear or worry that the past is going to come back to manipulate my present.

I can look at everything I've experienced and know that it's over. I've embraced it, I understand it, and I've learned from it. I forgive everything that kept me from achieving what it was that I wanted—including thoughts, experiences, and any memories. I forgive and accept myself. I love myself and know that I'm worthy of love. I respect myself and know that I'm worthy of respect.

Who do I want to be with forgiveness? I want to be that person who my spirit has known I was capable of becoming all along—someone who can fulfill her soul purpose and help as many people as possible. I want to—and will—live by what I know to be true and right. I will only enter into loving, kind, and honest relationships. I'll be a leader, showing others how they, too, can forgive themselves and others.

I love myself enough to nourish my body with healthy food, water, fresh air, and exercise. With forgiveness, I want to move into the freedom I desire and deserve so that I can open the door to infinite possibilities and create a life of my own design. I'm giving myself a fresh start and the chance to finally be me—to do the work that I came here to do. I'm free to live my life without the chains of the past making me fearful. I can move into the future with a clear conscience and a peaceful heart.

CHAPTER FOUR

THE KEY OF FREEDOM

USE THE KEY OF FREEDOM TO OPEN
THE DOOR TO A LIFE OF YOUR CREATION

> *Today is the beginning of a life of freedom.*
> *I choose today as my freedom day and*
> *celebrate it as the beginning of my growth.*

Choose to make today your freedom day. What is freedom? It's a place in your mind that says: *I'm not going to repeat negative patterns any longer. I'm capable of standing strong, and I'm not going back there. It doesn't* *matter what anyone else says. That's who I <u>was,</u> and their judgment of me no longer matters because I'm not that person any longer. I've changed inside, and I'm free of that old being.*

You *have* changed, so make a note of today's date. It's your new birth date—that of your authentic self. This is the beginning of your step forward. You've chosen to use the keys you acquired in the earlier chapters to release you from ego's control forever. You've decided that you're strong and that your ego can no longer battle you because you've opted to become who you know yourself to be. Celebrate yourself today and the energy that you're bringing into your life again. It's positive; it's growth.

> *Today, I'm born into my true self.*
> *I'm empowered by my truth.*

Celebrate yourself for everything you've accomplished so far. You've become aware of how ego has been controlling your mind. You've accepted who you were, who you are, and who you can become; and you've released negative judgments. You've learned how to forgive yourself, others, and the experiences of the past. You've learned that you're worthy of your own internal love. You've also uncovered the valuable lessons in the past and accept that today you're very capable of making your life a better place to be.

I'm capable of creating my perfect place.
I know I'm free to do so.

Now it's time for the next level of learning: you're ready to acquire the key of freedom, which allows you to open the door to a life of your own creation. It lets you stand—free from ego, judgment, and negativity from the past—and accept that the infinite possibilities are yours to create. Now that the burdens of past programming are no longer controlling your life and manipulating your mind, you're capable of having and creating anything you desire. It's very exciting!

I'm free to create anything I choose
without the burdens of the past controlling
and manipulating my mind.

Take the time to look within right now and ask yourself: *What do I want out of the rest of this life?* What do you want to have and to create? What are your dreams? As perfect as you already are, what changes do you want to make to become an even better, stronger, happier you? Now that the self-limiting thoughts are controlled, what do you want out of yourself and your future? You must love yourself enough to ask the questions and answer them based on what *you* desire—not based on ego or other people's goals.

Whatever you decide, you can make happen. In freedom, you can create anything. Know what you want and focus on it. Picture yourself taking all the steps necessary to get there. Imagine that you've achieved it already; see it in your mind as complete. Make that vision as clear as possible by keeping your mind free from your ego's control and by keeping your body as healthy as possible. Be consciously aware of the gift that you are and the gift that you're going to be. Do it for yourself. Nobody controls you. You're free to be yourself; you can choose what *you* want for your own life.

> *I choose to love my divine self through positive creation of my future. I know that I deserve all that I desire now that I'm free from the self-limiting thoughts of the past.*

What will it be? Are you going to choose the same negative patterns? Or are you going to opt to set out on the path of creation you've always wanted. Right now, you have the opportunity to change the outcome of your life. You can take a different path toward the future, which will alter the destination you seek. Figure out what you want.

My dreams are possible if I believe they are and allow myself freedom to create and enjoy them.

To help you discover what you want to create, try something new, something different. You might be surprised by what you're capable of doing. You could discover that you're an artist. You had no idea, but when you started painting and drawing, you realized that you were talented. Maybe you're a writer. Perhaps you knew this when you were little, but you blocked it out of your mind because a parent said, "Put that pen away; you're no good at writing." That's just an ego perception. Why not try again now that you're living without ego's controls? Create something out of joy, love, and self-expression that comes from your authentic self—from your spirit.

Maybe you already know what you want. You're aware of your purpose and you want to serve it every single day. When you create the steps necessary to carry this out, you're going to be graced with every opportunity to fulfill it. All that can stop you are your self-created limitations and boundaries, so get out of your own way.

Use the keys of *empowerment*—awareness, acceptance, and forgiveness—to let go of the fear, the limitations, and the boundaries. Use the keys to release your ego when it tries to tell you that it's easier to stay where you are. It will tell you not to use the key of *infinite possibilities*—the key of freedom—to walk through the door and into the life you really long to live because it's easier being dishonest, ignorant, self-centered, or whatever else is making you suffer.

I see now what keeps me unhappy; and I'm free
to change these habits, thoughts, and feelings. I
liberate myself from what was and create what will be.

The ego is wrong. It's not easier to stay where you are, to live with mental chaos and inner turmoil. It truly isn't. Sometimes it takes a lot of work to be free, but the ultimate reward is that you get to experience joy, peace, and happiness. Your mind is clear of guilt, dishonesty, fear, and ego manipulation. You get to go all the way to the very end of your life knowing that you did your best and became the person you were born to become. That's quite a reward, and it most certainly is worth the work.

Don't allow your ego to control you any longer. If you do, the opportunities available to you can become more difficult to see and to seize. Instead, allow your spirit to be in charge. Give your spirit—your true self— the freedom of control, and then everything becomes possible. You'll be free. There's nothing holding you back.

My past is a place I was. My present is a place I create. I control today and tomorrow.

The place to begin creating the person and the life you desire is in the now. The reality is that this moment is *all* that exists. You're in the *here-and-now;* it's where we all are. When tomorrow comes, you'll be here once again—and the day after that, and the day after that. You can create how your next *here-and-now* will look based on the choices you make in this very moment. If you choose poorly today by selecting a path or a lesson that's negative, then tomorrow will be created in a negative way. If you choose positively—to live in love, light, and honesty—your next *here-and-now* is going to be a better place, not only for you but for all those who surround you.

By evolving and creating the life you desire, everyone in your life is going to learn, for we all gain wisdom from each other. Live in honesty and those around you will grow from it; live in empowerment and those around you will learn that, too. They're in the moment with you, and it's producing a better place for them tomorrow as well.

> *I create my tomorrow by living happily,*
> *fearlessly, and freely today. I live <u>now.</u>*

This is the moment that counts. Today is the only day that you get to make the decisions that create your tomorrow. This is the time for your best choices, your best attempts to make tomorrow everything you want it to be. That way, when tomorrow becomes today, you'll have created something in which you feel really good—in which you feel strong, happy, and peaceful. You have this ability within yourself.

YOU'RE FREE TO CHOOSE YOUR THOUGHTS

> *Freedom is a place I create within my*
> *heart and mind before I share it.*

You're free to think that you're capable of creating whatever you want for your life. You're at liberty to believe that you're a good spirit, a good friend, or neighbor; you know who you are and that your beliefs are true. You're free to think that your truth is equivalent to everyone else's. That being said, know that what you think is what you create.

For instance, picture the kind of day you'll create if you wake up and think, *Oh no, I don't want to get up today. I'm too tired. I just want to stay in bed and sleep. I'll snuggle for another 30 minutes and then I'll get up*. When you finally roll out of bed, you say, "I want to stay in bed. I hate my stupid job. I don't look good." What you'll create is a negative and depressed day.

Yet how many people wake up and allow those kinds of thoughts to dominate their thinking every morning? Far too many! They're living in this sort of mind-set because they feel that nothing in their lives is worth getting up for. They're still choosing to live in the same negative pattern. They're not dwelling in freedom. They're not taking the steps to become who they want to be and to create lives of their own choosing.

My mind is mine to control. I'm now free from ego, and I give myself only positive thoughts and control.

You're capable of choosing a positive state of mind. You can wake up and think, *I'm not satisfied with my job or the excess weight that's affecting my health. I'm aware*

133

of that. I'm also aware that I'm capable in this moment of taking the steps to create a better tomorrow. The future will soon become today, so I'm going to take those steps right now. I'm going to do what I need to do to make tomorrow a positive, happy day. I'm not going to allow negative thoughts and feelings to control me. I choose my thoughts. I know what I want and what my purpose is—and I'm going to fulfill it.

What sort of experience do you think you'll create with these positive thoughts? It will be exactly what you imagined—a better day. You'll be stronger, more empowered, and free to walk on the path of your own choosing.

It's your choice whether you think positive thoughts or negative ones, whether they're controlled by ego or by your higher self. Knowing that you create each and every day within your mind, why not choose thoughts that serve you? One of the best things you can do for yourself is to maintain thoughts that allow you to create what you need to serve yourself and your purpose.

Today, begin preparing your every step for tomorrow. Hold the vision and focus of what you want. Choose to think that you can create that outcome. Affirm to yourself that you're capable of achieving all that you desire and of carrying out your purpose.

YOU'RE FREE TO BE WHO YOU WANT TO BE AND TO BECOME WHO YOU WANT TO BECOME

I now choose my future path based on my awareness, acceptance, and forgiveness of my true self without ego. I'm free to explore my options without fear. I create my future with admiration of my choices.

You have freedom no matter where you find yourself today. Maybe right now you're looking at your life and you're not happy with whom you've become. You're aware that your mother was an alcoholic and now you are, too; or your father was racist, and now you are, too. If that's not what you want to be, if you want something better for your life, you're free to change. Step into that privilege by using the first three keys of empowerment to gain the strength to change.

Use the key of *awareness* to release yourself from ego—to make yourself capable of breaking that pattern and of becoming the person you want to be. Use the key of *acceptance* to release negative judgments about yourself and others—to accept who you were, who you are, and who you can become. Use the key of *forgiveness* to forgive yourself of the past and to allow your mind to know that you truly are capable of making a fresh start. You deserve it.

Take control of your own mind. Acknowledge that what you're doing isn't serving you or others, nor is it something you truly want. Recognize that what you're doing isn't giving you anything you need to fulfill the purpose of your future. It's self-sabotage. Tell yourself, *No—it's over and done with. I'm capable of better.* Let your mind know that you can be anything you choose and that you don't have to repeat the negative patterns that the ego created. Accept that you've learned the lesson and forgive yourself.

I'm aware of the fact that today I want to accept my empowerment. I forgive the rationales I used to block this. I'm using my forgiveness to create freedom. I'm getting there tomorrow. I've made that choice today.

All who choose to forgive themselves and to stop negatively judging themselves for the way they were are capable of becoming who they want to become. When you receive awareness, acceptance, and forgiveness, you're then capable of also receiving freedom.

*I'm free to move around this world
and find the space that feels like home.
I create home from a place of freedom.*

If you aren't where you want to be right now, break the negative patterns and perceptions that tell you this is all you can do. You're capable of better. Suppose your grandfather was a ditch digger, your father was a grave digger, and now you're digging yourself into a hole. If that's not what you want out of life, let go of the beliefs that tell you it's all you can do. Stop digging yourself into a hole and start digging yourself out. Fill the abyss of the past and bury it behind you. Stand on top of it, make yourself capable of change, and never go back there. Begin following your spirit.

> *I follow my true spirit without the fear created by my ego; I'm free from this control for the rest of my life. I will always empower myself to be free.*

When you're following your spirit, every now and then your ego is going to try to regain the upper hand. It's as if it's saying: *I'm still here, and you're going to listen to me. How dare you try to control me? I've been in charge for your entire life, and I know the triggers that make you feel fearful. I know when you're down, when you're not 100 percent truly accepting of yourself, and when you're having a judgmental thought. Those are my doors to enter and regain power.*

Don't allow your ego to defeat you or take you away from the true focus of self and what you're learning.

When you feel your ego gaining power, remember that you hold the keys. Access them to allow your spirit—your true self—to regain control. Use them to lock out the ego and open the door to freedom once again. Step into that liberty and into the life you long to live.

I see unlimited possibilities in my vision of my future.

Focus on what you want to create and imagine the outcome before it arrives. See the steps you need to take to get you there, and begin taking them one at a time. You know where you need to go, so focus on it and don't let your ego control you anymore.

If you want to be the CEO of a company and not an employee, you can do that. Tell yourself: *I'm smart, I'm strong, and I'm going to get there. I'm going to start taking the steps.* If you're a clam digger and you realize now that you don't want to dig up clams—instead, you want to paint pictures on clam shells—then do it. Accept who you were, forgive yourself for not having the awareness sooner, and start living your life the way you want to.

YOU'RE FREE TO LIVE IN HONESTY

> *I live freely within my own mind, knowing*
> *that I'm doing so honestly. I'm living freely*
> *within truth to become the empowered, capable*
> *being that I want to be and that I know I can be.*

One of the biggest steps in freedom is being completely honest—with others and with yourself. Be frank with yourself about what you want and what you like. Perhaps you can truly say that you love dark chocolate and swimming, that it hurts you to see another person living in poverty, or that you love the world in which you live because you make it a better place.

It's crucial for you to be honest with yourself. To have a completely free life, you must know what you truly want. For instance, suppose you decide you want a better job. Be candid: Is it because you think it will make you more attractive? Don't pretend that you're something you know you don't really want to be. Always be real with yourself, and you'll have total freedom. You're capable of creating anything you want— just make sure it's what you truly desire.

What do you honestly want in your life right now? Do you want to live in a house that's worth millions of dollars? Would you like a home that's small and simple? In either case, if it's what your *spirit* longs for, and it's surrounded by love and free from judgment and ego, you can create it.

> *"Live your You." Truth is your birthright.*
> *Find your truth and empower yourself*
> *with it. You're free to focus on your true*
> *path, your true self, and your inner truth.*

You can create any outcome *you* choose if you put positive focus toward that outcome and you take the necessary steps to achieve it. Do you want to be the best metaphysical healer in the world? You can create that as long as you take the steps and keep going until you achieve it—but make sure you're doing it for *you.* Does your spirit long for you to be a television host? If it's not ego based but spirit driven because you need that to fulfill your purpose, then go for it—make it happen. You're capable of achieving what you desire.

In addition to being honest with yourself, be straightforward with others. You're free to speak your truth. Perhaps you find yourself standing in front of someone who's going on and on about how successful she is. If she asks whether or not you, too, see her as a success, it's okay to tell *your* truth. If you see her as unsuccessful because she continues to get involved in very unhealthy relationships, it's okay to say, "It seems that you're successful financially but it appears you're not successful emotionally." It's okay to say something like that because in speaking your truth, the other person will learn. It could lead to a dialogue that might end up helping the other person grow.

I live with honesty guiding my path.

We're not suggesting that you be rude and bluntly attack or insult others. Don't be like that. However, if you're asked to give an opinion, be honest. Suppose someone asks if you think they have an alcohol problem. If you do, you can say, "Yes, as a matter of fact I do, and I think you'd be better off if you took control of it." Why not be honest? This quality is often lost these days. It's almost like there's a truth phobia, which is fear driven. Sometimes you might lie so that you'll be accepted. However, the outcome is much better when you're honest because, in the end, you're not carrying around the guilt of dishonesty. Be candid with yourself and speak your truth—stay in freedom.

YOU'RE FREE TO FEEL PROUD OF YOURSELF

*I'm proud of who I am, who I was, and
who I'm becoming; every part of me deserves
empowerment. I'm proud of my true self.*

Once you've found freedom—once you experience it—you feel absolutely euphoric because anything is possible. It's not just a thought, it's a feeling. You can look in the mirror and say to yourself, *Wow! Way to go. I'm proud of you for not holding onto all of those things that were so negative. I'm proud of you for becoming aware of yourself and going through the steps necessary to become who you are now.* It's good to be proud of yourself; of the life you've created; and of being the loving, honest, and authentic you. That's a positive, healthy pride.

However, there's a negative aspect of pride, too— one that's driven by ego. This is the emotion that says: *I'm proud, and I'm cocky. This is me, and you're just going to have to accept it.* That sort of pride can stop you from having the freedom you desire. It can keep you from being able to forgive yourself and from discovering your authentic spirit. It definitely prevents you from accepting who you are.

I'm proud and driven by positive pride.
I'm accepting of my true self.

To discern between positive and negative pride, ask yourself: *Is this driven by fear or love?* Love is generated through the spirit, while fear is propelled by the ego. For instance, suppose you're feeling proud of yourself today for the changes you've made in your life. You're aware that you're basing those feeling on what you think about yourself. They're not dependent on whether anybody else thinks what you've done is important or unimportant. Your emotions spring from what you think and how you feel about what you've accomplished. That's self-love.

With positive pride, there are no comparisons involved; with negative pride, there are. Ego-driven arrogance thinks: *I'm better than you because of what I've accomplished. I'm more successful and smarter than you are.* That's driven by fear. The danger with this is that one day, when you're out comparing yourself with others, the ego will point out that you're not the best. It will say, *Hey, guess what? You're not so great after all. Look at her—she's better. Look at him—he's more than you'll ever be.* Your pride will turn to envy, anger, and an assortment of other negative feelings. Your ego will be in total control.

Sometimes the comparison isn't you against another person; it's you against yourself. Say, for instance, someone tells you: "You're so great at what you do." Pride gets hold of that and makes you feel inflated. Next time, somebody says, "Well, you're average." Pride makes you feel as though you've been insulted, and it hurts your feelings. Ego will creep back in and control you with thoughts such as: *Well, I don't like that person. I don't trust his opinion. He's a liar.* But maybe he was being honest. It could be that you weren't as great that day as you thought you were, or you weren't as good as you were the other time. Perhaps you're supposed to learn something from the comment that will help you become even better at what you do.

*I will not allow my ego to control my
ability to be proud of my true self.*

Instead, ego gets in the way and stops you from learning the lesson. On top of that, your ego is telling you: *He's right. You really aren't very good at all. In fact, you're pretty bad at what you do.* You're going to start doubting yourself. You'll feel a little more scared, a little more nervous. You're not going to feel as capable. It's a vicious cycle. Break the pattern by telling yourself:

I don't want or need to be living under ego-generated pride and fear. I'm free to live as myself, and it's sufficient.

Don't be afraid that letting go of these thoughts means you'll be unsuccessful. *Au contraire!* For those who can free themselves from the controls of the ego-generated pride, there are no limitations. You can rise to the top of any business. You can achieve anything in this world by being yourself. You break the cycles, you break the patterns, and you become free from boundaries. Use the keys of awareness, acceptance, and forgiveness to let go of ego-driven pride and to help you get back into freedom so that you can once again put yourself on the right path.

YOU'RE FREE TO CONTROL YOUR EGO

*I'm now capable of creating anything
I need. I'm free from ego's control and able
to create happiness, love, and abundance.*

You now know that you can do anything, be anything, and create anything. You're free. To stay in freedom, you need to be vigilant and look out for the occasions when ego attempts to regain control. One of those times is when you find yourself impressed with what you've achieved thus far. Your ego will stand in front of your accomplishment and tell you: *Ha! You've achieved nothing. You're a failure. You're useless. You're incapable of even thinking straight. How dare you attempt to become something that I know you can't be?*

Don't buy into that thought. Remember, it's only a perception that was created by your past, nothing more. Don't let it take you out of freedom. Accept that you're capable of creating everything you want.

Your ego will attempt to control you in some very obvious ways and, at times, in some very subtle ways. For instance, say you were given the chance to volunteer to help bring a gift to the troops overseas. Your spirit is happy and wants to do it, but your ego wants the credit and pipes up: *Sure, help the troops. You'll be seen as a local hero.* It's now taking away the joy of the spirit and replacing it with ego-driven pride. Helping others should be free of ego. Don't allow it to manipulate your spirit-driven act. Instead, allow your spirit to regain control by remembering you're doing this for others, not for yourself.

> *When ego tries to regain control, I remember the steps to get me back to my true freedom.*

Use the keys to release your ego and shift it around. Be thankful for the opportunity of knowing you're fulfilling your purpose as a giver. Remind yourself that this is *your* life, and you're free to live it authentically. Remember that this is a positive event. That way the ego won't be able to turn it around and take the negative approach. You'll be open to positive experiences and allow them to unfold in your life—without resentment, remorse, guilt, or fear. You'll know in your heart that these are opportunities that you need. You're simply projecting those needs and bringing the situations to you. They'll be positive, happy, loving, and exactly what you require to learn.

Here's another way the ego can try to stop you: Suppose you've made the decision to go to law school and become a lawyer. On the first set of exams, you receive only 52 percent. The ego may try to control you and get you questioning your ability to succeed. It will start telling you that the road is only going to get harder as it goes on. You'll wonder if you can actually achieve your goal. You'll remember comments made by others about how you'll never pull it off. The next thing you know, you're right back where you were at the beginning of this journey.

At that time, do the work again. Go through the thoughts and change their patterns. Get rid of the

negative ego and you'll succeed because you can create absolutely everything you want. Every detail—
emotional, physical, spiritual, psychological—you can
bring into being.

I know what I want, and I've made myself
capable of creating all that I need to be free.

Here's another example: Suppose you're long-
ing to meet someone with whom you can create a
relationship based on love and trust. You're recently
divorced and overweight, you have six children, and
you find yourself constantly thinking that you're
going to be alone for the rest of your life. You become
afraid of what others think, so every time you meet
someone, you turn the other way. You're afraid that
the other person is only going to see you as divorced
and fat, with six kids. That's because the ego is making you see yourself that way. If you turn away from
everyone, your ego will defeat you and your desire to
have a partner.

You're free to control your ego. Release the
thoughts; flip them around. Perhaps the facts are that
you're divorced, you have six kids, and you weigh more
than you'd like to. That's fine; you can still believe in
yourself. You can still accept that your children are

amazing and that anybody would be lucky to have them in his life. And know that you, too, are an incredible person.

*I no longer agree with everyone else's perception
of who I am. I'm able to change the way I feel and live
freely within my own opinion. I'm free to be me.*

With those thoughts in your mind, when someone looks your way, you might actually strike up a conversation. You might discover that the person you're talking with loves kids and always wanted a big family, but can't have children. Now you've created exactly what your heart desires. You've attracted it into your life because you know what's right for you. You aren't negative. You're not beating yourself up and destroying opportunities for your future. You're free to create all that you want. Discover what it is, control the ego, and watch your life unfold in magnificent ways.

*My path is clear now; my vision is bright and healthy.
I'm creating from a place of truth, love, and freedom.*

SELF-REFLECTION: WHAT DO I WANT TO CREATE IN MY LIFE NOW?

*Today I'm aware of my spirit's freedom. I'm free
from fear. I'm aware of my truth. I accept my identity.
I'm forgiven, and I have forgiven all. I'm free to love
myself, share my truth, and design my future.*

The key of freedom is now yours. You've learned that you're free to change your thoughts, to be who you want to be, and to become who you want to become. You've discovered that you're free to live in honesty, to feel proud of yourself, and to control the ego.

It's time to reflect on what you've just learned so that you can use this fourth key to open the door to a life of your creation. In this final letter—a letter of freedom—look within yourself to become more aware of what you want to create now that you know who you are without ego's control and have accepted and forgiven yourself and others.

Begin this letter with the following declaration of intention:

*My intention for this letter is to become more
aware of my freedom now that I live without
ego, judgment, and negativity from the past.*

150

With that intention in mind, write your answers to the following three questions:

- Who am I now that I'm free from ego, negative judgment, and the chains of the past?

- As perfect as I already am, what changes do I want to make to be a better me?

- Now that the self-limiting thoughts no longer control my life, what do I want for myself and my future?

You'll notice that this final example is much shorter than the previous three. This doesn't mean that *your* freedom letter needs to be short. In fact, each self-reflection you write can be any length that you need to express yourself. There's no set amount of words required.

Sample Letter of Freedom

Dear Self,

My intention for this letter is to become more aware of my freedom now that I live without ego, judgment, and negativity from the past.

151

My true self is now shining through; I'm no longer hidden. I live without fear of my own inner dialogue. I'm free of the self-limiting thoughts that caused me to be controlled, fearful, and riddled with guilt. I'm free to know who I am, and I love that person. The past training of my life no longer controls my every step. Now that I'm free, I'm more understanding and accepting of others and able to love unconditionally.

My life has direction, and I'm not afraid of where I'm going; I'm proud of the path I'm on. Being liberated from the past fears, guilt, and anxieties allows me to create a future of abundance, peace, and love. I'm so grateful that I'm able to experience this journey without ego's control.

Now that I've decided to free myself and move forward, I see that I want to take care of as many people as I can, helping them reach their own freedom and overcome their obstacles. I want to give everyone in the world the chance to embrace these lessons and understand what they've learned so they can be at my side as I grow and learn more without ego manipulating me.

I always believed that I was a good teacher and a wonderful healer. I'm now living the life I dreamed of. My goal is to become a doctor and to live without fear. I will become a doctor of natural medicine.

I'm proud that I live by my truth and that the past—as tough as it was—hasn't taken me away from being the person I knew I could be. I now understand that I can achieve everything I want. What I was taught in the past can't take anything away from me. I am free.

AFTERWORD

The Keys Are Within You

The four keys that allow you to open the door to true empowerment and infinite possibilities are within you.

You possess the key of *awareness* and can use it to free yourself from ego's control. You now know that ego is simply your inner dialogue telling you what you think about yourself, about others, and about the world. You realize that it's a perception of the mind created by other people's beliefs, opinions, and teachings. Its creation began when you were born and continued up to this very moment.

You own the key of *acceptance* and have learned how to use it to free yourself from negative judgments. You understand that judgment is how you perceive what other people think of you and how you view yourself based on that filter.

You hold the key of *forgiveness,* and you know how to use it to free yourself from the past. You're aware that you can't go back and change the past, but you can forgive yourself and others knowing that you've gained many lessons from those experiences.

You've acquired the key of *freedom* and know how to use it to open the door to a life of your creation. You understand that freedom means living without the burdens of the past controlling your life and manipulating your mind. You're free.

Use this book as your ongoing tool. It's something you're going to be able to reread and learn from again. Maybe this first time around the information that changed your life took the form of affirmations, such as: *I accept myself—mind, body, and spirit. I am perfect in this body that I have. I am growing and developing, and I am becoming who I am supposed to be. There is no ego here. I accept that I am worthy of my love.*

The second time you read the book, you might be struck by a connection you feel to the knowledge that suddenly hits you. You tell yourself: *That's right—I'm capable. I forgot about that piece of the puzzle. I'm going to get focused again on my steps forward. These are the choices I've made for myself, and my ego no longer controls me.*

The third time, you might be going through a new phase in your life, and you suddenly understand something in a way you hadn't before. Use the knowledge in the preceding pages to help you live in the freedom you deserve.

To stay in freedom, you must constantly check on the ego. Be on the lookout for those times when it will try to regain control—a financial setback, a marriage breakup, a friendship ending, and so on. These things happen. When they do, remember that as long as you're aware of the situation and aren't allowing the ego to control you, then you can accept it, forgive it, and free yourself from it. You can move forward knowing who you are and that you're capable of achieving all that you desire.

Also be prepared for the fact that even in freedom, guilt will slip back in every now and then. Why are you still being faced with guilt after all this work? That remorse might be telling you there's a lesson that you didn't learn completely, and you're in the position right now of potentially repeating the same experience. It's trying to put you back on the right path. That's not a negative—it's a positive. It's telling you: *Hold up and slow down. What you're about to experience is a repetition of the old identity—that inauthentic self that was so self-loathing and angry.*

Forgive the memory that's bringing the guilt—and forgive all those who may have been involved. Know that you've learned that lesson completely, and you're not going to go down that path again. Accept and love yourself, and break free from that pattern. You're living as your true self now; you're living authentically. Forgive yourself for what was, learn the lesson, and that guilt will go away.

Sometimes you might find that a certain issue—a certain fear—keeps coming back into your life. If this happens, go deeper into that one particular issue. Explore further and find out why it's controlling you. Discover where it's coming from. How does it keep getting back in, and why do you allow it to do so? What is it propelling? All fears exist for a reason. Anything that keeps re-creating itself after you've done the work is serving a purpose.

Do a little self-investigation to figure it out. Maybe it's a genuine fear that's protecting you from something that's going to occur. Perhaps it's prophetic, and you're supposed to take action. If that's the case, follow your intuition and act.

What do you do, on the other hand, if you determine that the reason this fear has returned is that you've allowed ego to regain control? What then? Do you go back and start the work of becoming aware, accepting, and forgiving all over again? Do you go back through the building blocks and do the releasing again? You're darn right you do. Every time ego gets a bit of control, you need to stop, become aware, gain acceptance, and allow forgiveness in order to return to freedom.

Your journey began in the opening pages of this book, and you now have the keys to continue on this path for the rest of your life. Use the keys . . . and enjoy everything you're about to create.

ACKNOWLEDGMENTS

From Denise Marek:

To my dear daughters, Lindsay and Brianna—I love you both so very much. Thank you for the incredible joy, love, and laughter you bring to my life. I'm so proud of the kind, strong, loving women you're becoming. Thank you for your patience as Sharon and I wrote this book; and for loving, encouraging, and inspiring me every step of the way. I wish for you to always know who you truly are, to follow your hearts, and to live your authentic lives.

I also thank Terry Marek. We brought two terrific daughters into this world, and I'm so grateful that you've been the loving father to them that you have. I appreciate you, and I wish you much love and happiness.

To Sharon Quirt I give my heartfelt gratitude. It's been quite a journey over the last few years. Thank you for guiding and supporting me along the way and helping me discover my own inner self and strength.

I'm honored to have co-authored this book with you, and even more honored to be your friend.

For my family: You've each contributed to the lessons and experiences that have shaped me into who I am today, and I'm grateful for each and every one of you. In alphabetical order, I extend my profound gratitude to Jim and Joan Allcock, Courtney Forbes, Murray and Betty Forbes, Murray and Laura Forbes, Bob and Jo-Anne Kite, Marion Kite, Deanna and Ted Thomas, Erin Thomas, and Nicholas Thomas. I also thank the Forbes, Geris, and Neabel families. I love you all!

My heartfelt thanks to my friends: Melissa and Nash Annan—thank you for your encouragement and the gift of laugher (I think I need more cowbell). Dan Carter and Paula Beebe—I can't even begin to tell you how much your friendship means to me; I love you both. Jim Estill—I give thanks to you for your direction and guidance; as busy as you are, you've always been there to help me keep focused (back to work). Alison Fleming—thanks for your positive energy; it ripples out and has enriched my life. Burt Henderson—I value your friendship, and I'm thankful to have you in my life. Mike Peleshok—perfect timing! Thanks for your excitement, energy, and ideas. Michael Shire—I'm so glad you found your talent and that you share it with others. That's a gift. Deanna Thomas—wow!

I feel so lucky to have a sister who's also such a terrific friend. I'm so very thankful for your support, love, and encouragement. You're beautiful inside and out, and I love you very much.

I extend deep appreciation to Marlene Jobb, Rob McGlashan, Caitlin Jobb, Dave Stone, Alex Jobb, and Ethan Jobb. You're a terrific family, and I'm honored to have you as my friends. Your kindness, generosity, and care have deeply touched my heart. I'll be forever thankful for all of you and the significant difference you've made in my life and in my daughters' lives.

I'd also like to thank three outstanding women who make the world a better place—Robin Dines, Beth McBlain, and Debbie McCoy. I just love you all to pieces. Thanks for your vision, energy, warmth, and compassion. I send my love and light to you all.

A huge thank-you to our outstanding editing team: Heather Anderson, Katherine Coy, Jessica Kelley, Jill Kramer, and Catherine Leek.

Finally, I extend special and abundant gratitude to Reid Tracy at Hay House. Because of your belief in this project, *The Keys* will now be able to make its way into the hands of all those individuals who are searching for a life of true empowerment and infinite possibilities. From the bottom of my heart—thank you!

From Sharon Quirt:

My deepest gratitude and acknowledgement is made to the following people: I start out with my son, Eric, who came to me at a time when my life was fiercely controlled by my ego. He was God-sent, and an angel to me from the day of his birth: May 18, 1984. I admit that all I know about unconditional love comes from his presence in my life. Thank you, Eric. You've taught me so very much in this lifetime. Without you, I'm sure that the road would have taken a much less empowered direction. I love you, Eric, with all of my heart. I'm so proud to be your mom.

To Denise Marek, for allowing me to share this journey of knowledge with you—to teach you and guide you and to be part of your most wonderful life. I'm so proud of you, Denise, and I'm grateful to have the chance to be your friend and business partner. Thank you, Denise, for being the best business partner I've ever known. I look forward to a long, happy journey together. I admire you and love you very much. Thank you to your girls for allowing me to have so much of your time to write this book—you're both angels.

To Ken Chartrand: You came into my life at a time when I needed to learn what freedom truly meant. From an emotional standpoint in a relationship, I've never felt free. Now in your love, I am free. Thank you for being my best friend and teaching me unconditional love on a level I've never known. I love you: one man, one woman, forever.

To Louise Hay, for all the wisdom you've shared with me through your books, CDs, and seminars. You are truly an inspiration.

To Susan Weaver and Tammy Gould, two of my favorite women in this world, for all the times you helped me feel better about myself and stronger, and to know that I am worthy of true friendship. I'm so grateful to you both.

ABOUT THE AUTHORS

Denise Marek is known as "The Worry Management Expert." An international speaker, author of *CALM: A Proven Four-Step Process Designed Specifically for Women Who Worry* (Hay House, 2006), and television personality, she has helped hundreds of thousands of individuals transform their feelings of worry into feelings of inner peace, gain the confidence to take risks, and re-create their lives. Denise hit the speaking circuit full-time in 1997. AIG, American Express, Assante Advisory Services, Canada Revenue Agency, and Toyota are among the many corporations, government agencies, financial institutions, and professional groups that have hired Denise to speak at their events. In June 2001, Denise earned the coveted Toastmasters International Accredited Speaker Award for Professionalism and Outstanding Achievements in Public Speaking. She lives in Ontario, Canada.

Website: **www.denisemarek.com**

Sharon Quirt counsels individuals worldwide, including the United States, Canada, United Kingdom, Italy, France, and South America, helping them rediscover the art of living joyfully and with purpose. Her life experience; extensive educational background (from metaphysics to studies in law, medicine, and business); and keen intuitive insight have gifted Sharon with the ability to teach, understand, and speak her truth. Having learned to listen to her inner self and become empowered by her strengths, she's become free from ego and lives a life of happiness, abundance, and peace. She resides in Ontario, Canada.

Website: **www.sharonquirt.com**

Keynotes, Seminars, and Workshops

Authors, keynote speakers, business consultants, and facilitators, Denise Marek and Sharon Quirt have more than 20 years of experience with top companies and associations around the world. Individually, they've presented programs internationally on leadership, personal power, life balance, stress reduction, worry management, effective communication, and attitude management with groups ranging in size from 10 to 10,000 people.

Together, Denise and Sharon are two dynamic presenters who will empower you and your organization to move forward. Through firsthand demonstration of the principles of empowerment, they'll instill positive and lasting changes in the attitudes, actions, teamwork, and relationships in your organization. They'll help you attain personal and professional success.

To book Denise Marek and Sharon Quirt
for your next conference or in-house event, visit:
www.denisemarek.com or **www.sharonquirt.com**

We hope you enjoyed this Hay House book. If you'd like to receive our online catalog featuring additional information on Hay House books and products, or if you'd like to find out more about the Hay Foundation, please contact:

Hay House, Inc.
P.O. Box 5100
Carlsbad, CA 92018-5100

(760) 431-7695 or **(800) 654-5126**
(760) 431-6948 (fax) or **(800) 650-5115 (fax)**
www.hayhouse.com® • **www.hayfoundation.org**

Published and distributed in Australia by: Hay House Australia Pty. Ltd., 18/36 Ralph St., Alexandria NSW 2015 • *Phone:* 612-9669-4299 *Fax:* 612-9669-4144 • www.hayhouse.com.au

Published and distributed in the United Kingdom by: Hay House UK, Ltd., 292B Kensal Rd., London W10 5BE • *Phone:* 44-20-8962-1230 • *Fax:* 44-20-8962-1239 • www.hayhouse.co.uk

Published and distributed in the Republic of South Africa by: Hay House SA (Pty), Ltd., P.O. Box 990, Witkoppen 2068 • *Phone/Fax:* 27-11-467-8904 • orders@psdprom.co.za • www.hayhouse.co.za

Published in India by: Hay House Publishers India, Muskaan Complex, Plot No. 3, B-2, Vasant Kunj, New Delhi 110 070 • *Phone:* 91-11-4176-1620 • *Fax:* 91-11-4176-1630 • www.hayhouse.co.in

Distributed in Canada by: Raincoast, 9050 Shaughnessy St., Vancouver, B.C. V6P 6E5 • *Phone:* (604) 323-7100 *Fax:* (604) 323-2600 • www.raincoast.com

<u>Take Your Soul on a Vacation</u>

Visit **www.YouCanHealYourLife.com**® to regroup, recharge, and reconnect with your own magnificence. Featuring blogs, mind-body-spirit news, and life-changing wisdom from Louise Hay and friends.

Visit **www.YouCanHealYourLife.com** today!